Beyond the Pink Moon

A Memoir of Legacy, Loss and Survival

By

Nicki Boscia Durlester

for my mother

Table of Contents

barn's burnt down...now i can see the moon.

- Masahide, 17th Century

1   CLOCKWORK

Spring break was over and my children were headed back to college. My daughter, Ally, had two months until graduation and my son, Matt, was finishing his freshman year. They both attended my alma mater, Franklin & Marshall College in Lancaster, Pennsylvania. It was a source of great pride and provided peace of mind knowing big sis was there in case baby bro needed her. I was delighted they were gaining exposure to my Pennsylvania roots. Having grown up in a suburb of Los Angeles, Amish country was a world away from their life of privilege in Lalaland.

I have never been able to drop Ally and Matt off curbside at the airport. I still walk them in and hang on to every glance until they disappear out of sight. Then I boohoo all the way back to the car. It is the same ritual I engaged in when they went off to nursery school. For days I prepared them for their big separation from mama bear, certain the transition would be difficult. When the first day of school finally arrived I was the only one with tears streaming down my face. Separation anxiety has always been my Achilles heel. People are their childhoods and mine had been fraught with goodbyes.

As I accompanied Ally and Matt to the security checkpoint at LAX, I felt a wave of nostalgia for days gone by. It seemed like just yesterday I was walking them into school, one on each hand. Time had flown by in the blink of an eye. Now they were on the opposite coast and the goodbyes were more difficult. I would begin counting the days until summer vacation. Little did I know those days would be filled with life-changing events for me.

I had scheduled my annual mammogram for the day after they left. Like clockwork, I tried to make my appointment on or around the same day every year. Besides being prudent, it was an obsessive-compulsive thing. I experienced a lot of anxiety in the preceding weeks as I typically did before my annual checkup. Truth be told, I had been living under a dark cloud since I was five years old when my mother was diagnosed with breast cancer. It was 1962, long before women blew the lid wide open on the disease. My mother, Bianchina Buschi Boscia, was forty-three years old.

2   ITSY BITSY SPIDER

One of my earliest memories is of my mother slowly crawling her fingers up the kitchen wall. At the time I thought she was playing Itsy Bitsy Spider. I would sing along in amusement as she struggled to reach as high as she could. I had no idea she was trying to strengthen her right arm, which had been ravaged by a radical mastectomy.

I vividly remember the day she came home from the hospital. I can still see her coming through the front door, wearing a light colored dress highlighting her tiny waist and hourglass figure. As she walked through our wood paneled vestibule my father warned me not to hug her too tight. I was lying on the green velvet couch in our living room, the one reserved for special occasions, recovering from a terrible case of chicken pox. As she gingerly sat down next to me I leaned over and gave her a gentle hug. She had the softest skin in the world and always smelled like Shalimar. I was so relieved and happy to have her home. I had missed her terribly during her ten days in the hospital. What a difference a half century makes; today a woman is lucky if her insurance company approves a forty-eight hour stay in the hospital after undergoing a mastectomy. It borders on the criminal.

I cannot recall the first time I saw the scarred landscape where her breast used to be. Her chest on the right side was concave and a significant part of the underside of her upper arm was missing. My mother never hid from me. She seemed unfazed by her disfigurement. She would insert an inflatable prosthesis into her bra as if it was no big deal. Every once in a while she would get what she called "a flat tire". It happened one Sunday at church. In the middle of mass, as I sat next to her, she let out an audible, "Uh oh!" When I looked over, she glanced down and surreptitiously pointed to her chest. She was wearing a gray and white dress, which matched her thick wavy hair always swept up in a French twist. A devilish grin spread across her face. She could see the humor in any situation, providing a layer of protection for my brother and me. As young children, we had no idea how closely she danced with death. Years later she confessed she had initially been given a bleak prognosis, but cancer had never met a relentless opponent like my mother. She was the original woman warrior.

3 LA FAMIGLIA

My mother hailed from a big Italian family. Her parents, Antonio and Carolina Buschi, emigrated from Corropoli, Italy, passing through the port of New York at Ellis Island before moving to Martins Creek, a small town in eastern Pennsylvania settled predominately by Italian immigrants.

In typical Roman Catholic fashion they began churning out babies until their brood reached a whopping eleven children, including three sons, Armando, Orville and John, and eight daughters, Ann, Bianchina, Helen, Lydia, Emma, Elizabeth, Mary and Edna. Combined, the siblings would have thirty-four children between them.

I have often wondered: if my grandfather knew he carried the gene that would devastate his family, would he and my grandmother have had so many children? In the early years there was no foreshadowing of what was to come. When he was diagnosed with lung cancer in his mid-fifties it was attributed to his work at the cement mill. It seemed logical all the dust he inhaled had been the culprit.

Years later, when seven of his daughters were stricken by breast, ovarian and fallopian tube cancer, the doctors began to connect the dots pointing in the direction of a cancer cluster caused by environmental toxins or genetically linked malignancies. Six of the seven daughters diagnosed with cancer would eventually lose their battles with the insidious disease. Only one daughter escaped cancer's clutches. In an ironic twist, years later she would be diagnosed with Alzheimer's disease. While her sisters lost their bodies to a malignant enemy, she lost her mind and all of her sorrowful memories. Perhaps a blessing in disguise.

The sole survivor, my Aunt Lydia, was diagnosed with post-menopausal early stage breast cancer at the age of sixty-seven, a less aggressive form of the disease, which increased her chances for survival. She is eighty-five years old and has lived long enough to see her older daughter die of lung cancer at the age of fifty-nine. Life can be heartbreaking.

It was profoundly sad when my mother lost her first sister to breast cancer. My Aunt Emma was forty and she left behind four children; the youngest was five. She lived in Harrisburg, Pennsylvania, one hundred miles away from us. My mother and father were walking out the door to visit her when the phone rang. My father quickly answered and from the glum look on his face, my mother knew it was too late. Emma had died. Mom threw herself on the couch and cried out in unbearable pain and anguish. I was seven years old. It left an indelible imprint of sadness on my soul.

My mother's three brothers were plagued by illness as well. Her younger brothers, Orville and John, were diagnosed with prostate cancer, which has also been linked to the BRCA (breast cancer) gene. Her oldest brother, Armando, had a blood disease that was thought to be a precursor to leukemia. In the years to follow, it was confirmed there was a genetic link with most of the malignancies in the Buschi family, speculated to have been passed down from their father, who lost his life to lung cancer at the age of fifty-eight.

In the late 1970s the Buschis and their offspring were invited to participate in a study at the National Institutes of Health (NIH) with the goal of identifying the gene that contributed to the staggering number of cancer cases in the family. I say 'contributed' because a person's genetic makeup alone cannot cause cancer. There has to be another factor such as environment, diet, stress, a compromised immune system, among others to trigger the disease. Over a hundred families participated in the NIH study (which continues to this day) and ours is the third largest, with the most comprehensive data. In 2001, after more than two decades of research, the Buschi family gene was finally identified as BRCA2. Each family member has a fifty-fifty chance, a coin toss, of carrying the gene. I lost the toss, which meant I have a greater risk of getting cancer than the general population, and worse may have passed it on to my children. It is not the legacy I want to leave my daughter and son. I hope and pray it ends with me.

4 TRENDSETTER

My mother was a woman ahead of her time, setting health trends before they were in vogue. When she read there were clinics in Mexico dispensing laetrile treatments to cancer patients with successful outcomes, she devised a way to incorporate it in her diet. She began her day with a homemade concoction of foods rich in laetrile, guzzling a shake of brewer's yeast, raw eggs, apricot kernels and bitter almonds, convinced it might lead to health and longevity. Each morning she did her exercises and would squeeze in a walk as often as she could, sometimes dragging me along for company. As much as I disliked exercising I loved that one-on-one time with my mother. I would walk with my arm linked through hers and she would listen intently as I babbled on about the trivial things in my life. The woman was a saint.

Our home was a humble half-double with one bathroom in a modest neighborhood in Easton, Pennsylvania, the same house my father had lived in since he was eighteen. My Aunt Elizabeth, my mother's younger sister, lived with us for several years when I was growing up. My parents furnished a room for her in our attic. Aunt Liz was our babysitter. She was also my sponsor for my Catholic confirmation, when I was given the middle name of Elizabeth, after her. She worked as a secretary at Dixie Cup, smoked like a chimney, never married and died of ovarian cancer at the age of thirty-nine. I was nine years old.

The last time I saw her was on Easter Sunday. My mother made my talk-of-the-town Easter outfits every year and she wanted Aunt Liz to see her latest creation. I had a Jackie O inspired pink dress and coat with a little pillbox hat to match. Aunt Liz had been rushed to the hospital shortly before and we all knew without saying a word that she would not be coming home. I don't think she knew I was there, but I knew. She died eleven days later, on April 21, 1966. It was a tragic loss for our family, and it would be years before I ventured up to the attic without feeling an overwhelming sense of sadness and loss.

5   MANGIA!

My mother, the original multitasker, figured out a way to do it all. She was up at the crack of dawn making breakfast, packing homemade lunches and often walking us to school. We lived several blocks from St. Anthony's, our Catholic elementary school. Between my mother and the Salesian Sisters, my brother and I did not have a chance. No getting away with any shenanigans in our house. Whether we needed it or not, Mom got out the metal spoon a couple of times a year just to keep us in line. Nothing like old fashioned discipline and fear to keep you on the straight and narrow. One look from my mother could stop you dead in your tracks. She had that gift of the Italian evil eye.

She also had the gift of cooking. She seemed happiest making a fresh pot of sauce for our Sunday spaghetti and meatballs ritual. The aroma and sizzle of garlic frying still triggers some of my fondest memories. On Sunday morning we would attend mass as a family, and then sit down to dinner in the early afternoon. Later in the day Mom and I would stand around the kitchen and pick at the leftovers.

I feel as though I spent half my childhood running to the local A & P for last minute ingredients for something she was concocting. It was always worth it in the end, when we sat down as a family to one of her mouth-watering feasts, accompanied by a hard crusted loaf of Italian bread and homemade wine. While other kids were eating bologna sandwiches on

Wonder Bread, we had Mom's homemade meatball sandwiches for lunch. No processed foods for us. Our refrigerator looked like a work of art, packed with the freshest of foods and always brimming over with something good to eat. You couldn't walk into our house without my five feet, three-inch mother shoving a plate in front of you. Mangia! It's an Italian mantra. And if you didn't devour every morsel, she would take it as a personal affront.

Mom had one small oven in her tiny kitchen and another ancient one in the basement. When she wasn't in the kitchen cooking up a storm we always knew where to find her. Bianchina's basement was her secret hideaway. She never complained that she didn't have a bigger kitchen or the latest cooking tools. She made it work with what she had.

Mom was also an extraordinary seamstress, a voracious reader, and a magician with a pair of knitting needles. She could knit and crochet at breakneck speed. When I was in college she made me a sweater that was the envy of my friends. Brown and beige with a shawl collar and wooden buttons, I wore that sweater everywhere I went and kept it in a safe place for years to come. When my daughter experienced her first winter in Pennsylvania, I dug out that sweater made by the grandmother she never knew and shipped it to her as a surprise with a personal note. It gave me great comfort knowing we both wore that sweater while walking the grounds of the same college campus, decades apart, with my mother's loving workmanship wrapped around us.

By the time I was ten, Mom had been cancer-free for five years. Ten years out she was still going strong and we all believed she was in the clear. She never seemed to skip a beat, and we gratefully shared those ten holiday seasons celebrating our favorite time of year.

Our Christmas Eve celebration was the highlight of the holidays in the Boscia household. Mom began baking in November for the big event. She was famous for her chocolate rocks (her secret recipe), sesame cookies, and rum fruitcakes, stored in big aluminum tins that lined our attic stairs. My favorites were the Italian lace cookies with pink icing and multicolored sprinkles. I would quietly sneak and grab a few, leaving a path of crumbs that would get me snagged every time.

My mother would cook for weeks in preparation of the Italian seven fish feast. She soaked the bacala in water for days to remove the excess salt, keeping it on the frigid upstairs porch until she deemed it ready to be cooked in her delicious tomato sauce with potatoes. The menu included scungilli, calamari, smelts, and other delicacies of the sea. Her signature dish was her homemade manicotti, light and fluffy; it melted in our mouths. Every holiday dinner began with a first course of mama's manicotti and ended with her incomparable ricotta cheesecake.

Christmas Eve continues to be the biggest night in my home. It's a wee bit different, considering the fact that I married Big Al, a conservative Jew from New Haven, Connecticut. Oy vey! Although we agreed to raise our children Jewish, Christmas is the one tradition of mine Big Al insisted we keep. He knows how important it is to me and he can't hide the fact he loves it too. I used to take such pleasure watching him struggle with the Christmas lights; he was all thumbs. It just isn't in his DNA.

I will always cherish the first Christmas in our new home, the California ranch we said we would live in for three years. Twenty-three years later, we're still happily there. Ally was ten months old and Matthew was just a gleam in our eyes. As I stood before our kitchen window, facing our cul-de-sac, I saw Big Al drive up with a Christmas tree tied on top of his red Jeep Cherokee. It was a Charlie Brown tree, the most beautiful one I had ever seen. We strung together popcorn and cranberries and made red bows out of ribbon. Ally crawled around us squealing in delight.

That was the start of a Durlester family tradition. With each passing year the holiday has grown in size and scope. Right after Thanksgiving, I transform our house into Santa's Village. We now have two fresh trees, which Ally decorates to the nines. Big Al no longer hangs the lights. We hire someone to make our house the most garish one in our Jewish neighborhood. Matthew's job is to dole out compliments to his mama bear and big sis for a job well done. And on Christmas Eve we celebrate with fifty or so of our closest Jewish friends and do it up Italian style. The favorite item on the menu is always Bianchina's cheesecake.

6 DEVOTION

I was fifteen and a sophomore in high school when Mom began bleeding inexplicably. She had gone through early menopause shortly after her mastectomy, so it seemed odd she would suddenly get her period again. Her gynecologist performed a D & C (dilation and curettage), and for a short time everything was fine. When the bleeding resumed, she had a second D & C, successfully treating the problem for an additional few months. When her symptoms recurred again, her doctor recommended exploratory surgery to make a definitive diagnosis. That was back in the day before MRIs or CAT scans, when surgery was frequently used as a diagnostic tool.

We were devastated when Mom was diagnosed with fallopian tube cancer. It was a second primary cancer unrelated to the breast disease she had battled a decade earlier. Almost thirty years later we would learn both cancers were linked to her BRCA2 gene.

My father told my brother and me the news while Mom was still in the hospital. When I went to visit her, I did my best to keep a stiff upper lip. After all she had been through, she always had a smile on her face and not an ounce of self-pity.

She would begin chemotherapy shortly after leaving the hospital. It was traumatic seeing my mother suffer through the treatments and lose her hair. She would be violently ill for the first twenty-four hours after chemo; it was much harsher back then. My father was incredibly devoted to her, and never left her side. I would hear them stumbling around the house at night as they went back and forth from their bedroom to the bathroom. I don't know how my dad did it, considering he worked two jobs. He never complained, nor did she.

Shortly after chemo ended, her hair grew back thicker than ever and she seemed to bounce back easily from her ordeal. We all hoped she beat cancer for a second time. For three years she was strong and healthy and everything seemed to return to normal, but life would have other plans for all of us.

During the fall of my freshman year in college, Mom's cancer reared its ugly head again. She endured a second round of chemo to treat her advancing cancer, and I returned home to a mother weakened from treatments. She lost her hair again and had the pallor of someone fighting metastatic disease. She would win her third battle against cancer, but the war would continue.

7   ROAD TRIP

Mom loved to take a ride. Her favorite was a Sunday afternoon drive along Route 611, a winding road that hugs the banks of the Delaware River from Easton to her hometown of Martins Creek. She enjoyed visiting old friends and driving by the Buschi homestead, long since sold and dilapidated from years of neglect. She was always looking for someone to go with her and I loved riding shotgun.

It was no surprise that my mother wanted to jump on the bandwagon when I told my parents I wanted to go to Florida over spring break of my junior year in college. Not quite the wild time I had imagined. While other college students were driving to Ft. Lauderdale in caravans, my boyfriend, Mark, and I had my parents as chaperones. My father and Mark shared the driving as we made our way to Lake Placid in central Florida. My Aunt Lydia, my mother's younger sister, had a vacation home there and my parents stayed with her while Mark and I drove on to Miami Beach.

Mom seemed strong and happy on the way down, excited to be visiting her favorite sister, Lydia. She had been enjoying a period of good health the past couple of years, after rebounding from her most recent round of chemotherapy. She seemed to be proving her doctors wrong regarding her prognosis. Halfway through the trip back to Pennsylvania she began complaining of back pain. I began to worry it might be something serious. Mom tried to put on a happy face, but I knew she was suffering. Mark and I went back to school to finish the semester and my parents continued the drive home. In the following days, she would find out her cancer had returned with a vengeance.

I did not see her again until the Saturday before Mother's Day. My brother and I went home for family dinner to celebrate the holiday. My grandmother, Nanny Stella, was there along with my brother's fiancée, Diane. By now, Mom had lost her hair for the third time from her resumed chemotherapy treatments. She was wearing a scarf, but generally looked in good health. She made an incredible feast and we gathered around the dining room table as a family for the last time.

As we were doing the dishes, she pulled me into the laundry room off the kitchen. I remember exactly where we were standing, by our back door, and I can still see the concerned look in her tired eyes.

"What's the matter Mom?" I gently asked.

She began to cry. "I am so tired, Nicki. Tired of reaching. I wish you were settled. I still worry about you."

I told her not to worry and reassured her she would be all right. After all, she had battled cancer for fifteen years. She was invincible and could survive anything. Inwardly, I was concerned this time might be different.

Once she gathered herself, we said our goodbyes, knowing I would be home in two weeks when finals ended.

That night, just as I got back to school, my father called to tell me he had taken Mom to the hospital. I was sitting on my bed on top of the pink and red flowered bedspread she had made for me. Matching curtains hung on the windows of my room. I wondered if this would be like all the other times she had gone to the hospital; however, this time would prove to be different. She never came home.

My mother lived long enough to see my brother and me grow up, but not long enough for us to enjoy her indomitable spirit and extraordinary grace. She died May 25, 1977 at 8:08 in the morning, the day before my brother graduated from medical school and ten days before he got married. I was by her side, holding her hand when she peacefully passed away. As I left her hospital room I turned and saw my father kissing her on the lips goodbye. I remember thinking he would not be able to live without her. They had been happily married for twenty-eight years and he had stood by her side in the best and worst of times. I could never have predicted that seven months later I would be standing next to my brother, in front of a Justice of the Peace, witnessing my father's marriage to his second wife. Life goes on.

We buried my mother the next morning and drove straight to Jerry's graduation. When I look at the photographs from that day, placed carefully within our family album, there is barely a hint we had just come from my mother's funeral. We are all beaming in the graduation pictures, hugely proud of the first doctor in our family. The preceding page in the album includes a picture of Mom and Dad on the beach in Florida, taken just two months before while on the spring break trip. She and Dad are standing side by side next to a tree, his hand resting lovingly on her shoulder. They're both grinning broadly as they pose for the camera, unaware this would be the last picture they would take together. One page she was here, and the next she is glaringly gone, perfectly illustrating the fleeting nature of life.

I have always believed my mother let go so she could be with us in spirit. There was no way she was going to miss her beloved son's big day. And when he married Diane ten days later, there was no doubt she was in that church with us. When the lights flickered during their vows we knew she was there giving her blessing. She was a truly remarkable woman who, in the words of our priest, taught us not only how to live, but how to die with unwavering faith and dignity.

8 LEGACY

On Monday, March 23, 2009, the day after spring break ended, I had a 10:00 a.m. date with destiny. My annual visit with the radiologist always brought back thoughts of my mother. It had been almost thirty-two years since she passed away. At fifty-two, I had lived much more of my life without her. It was hard to believe she was nine years younger than I when she was diagnosed with breast cancer.

As I drove to my radiologist's office I wondered what this year's mammogram would show. The night before, I told Big Al I had a bad feeling. We were lying on opposite sides of our favorite u-shaped couch in our family room.

He glanced over at me with a look of impatience and repeated words he had often said to me, "You've been dying since the day I met you. You're not going anywhere. You'll outlive us all."

I had never found those words comforting, nor was I looking for a response. I just needed to think out loud.

I had been Dr. Pritchard's patient for twenty-two years. Mammogram day had always proved to be lucky for me. A negative test result brought a sigh of relief for another year of good health. For twenty-one years I had received positive news and felt incredibly blessed. But there were some curve balls along the way.

In 2001, when I found out I had the BRCA2 gene, I gave serious consideration to having prophylactic mastectomies. I met with several specialists, including Dr. Armando Giuliano, the renowned Director of the John Wayne Cancer Institute at St. John's Hospital in Santa Monica. He was the most direct. He looked me straight in the eye and asked me if I would prefer getting a breast cancer diagnosis someday versus doing something to prevent it now. Profound words of wisdom which I would choose to dismiss. The odds were definitely stacked against me considering the fact that my chances of getting breast cancer increased over time; however, there was also a slim possibility it might not happen. At the time I had two young and very busy children, a business to run, a home to manage, and the list goes on and on. Taking time out for major surgeries, including the mastectomies and reconstruction, seemed daunting. I also knew I would still have a 2-3% chance of getting breast cancer even if I had the mastectomies; much less than the general population, but still at risk. No decision was black or white.

In an ironic twist, I was diagnosed with multiple sclerosis in 1991 and was concerned a major surgery might further compromise my immune system. My MS had been in remission for years and I wanted it to stay that way.

To make matters worse, sadly, my father passed away in 1991 of colon cancer, another genetically linked disease. Removing my colon was clearly out of the question. Just as I would rely on a colonoscopy every five years to screen for colon cancer, I would do the same with the screening techniques available for breast cancer. My gynecologist informed me that breast cancer typically appeared later in the offspring of BRCA2 carriers, so I felt as though I had time to reconsider my decision. At some point you have to get on with your life. But Dr. Guiliano's words would continue to haunt me.

In the meantime, I would be more vigilant about my health. I would have an annual mammogram and ultrasound along with monthly self-breast exams, and visits to my gynecologist every six months for checkups. I would also have a baseline MRI with a follow-up three months later to get the closest thing to a 360-degree picture of my breasts. Additionally, I would take a holistic approach to my health and do whatever I could to stave off cancer, including maintaining a positive attitude, a well balanced diet, exercise and healthy lifestyle. Throw in some acupuncture, vitamins, Chinese herbs, therapeutic massage and cranial sacral sessions and maybe, just maybe, I could beat the odds.

Besides, I had already given at the bank, big time. In 1990, prior to being tested for the gene, at the age of thirty-four, when Ally was four and Matthew only eleven months, I had a total hysterectomy including removal of my ovaries due to my family history of ovarian cancer. I lacked confidence in the limited and unreliable screening techniques for ovarian cancer. I felt like a ticking bomb, and more than anything wanted to see my children grow up.

There is never, however, a free lunch in life. Although removing my ovaries greatly decreased my risk of ovarian cancer, my gynecologist told me the loss of estrogen produced by my ovaries could adversely affect my heart and bones. My dilemma was whether or not to take hormone replacement therapy (HRT). At thirty-four, I believed I was too young to be thrown into full-blown menopause. So I took Premarin (synthetic estrogen) and kept taking it for eighteen years.

Every six months when I visited my gynecologist for a checkup I would ask him the same question. "Is it safe to be on HRT?"

His answer never changed.

"There are no conclusive studies that demonstrate estrogen alone increases a women's risk of breast cancer. Conversely there have been studies that have shown that estrogen alone can reduce the risk of breast cancer in women who carry the BRCA2 gene."

I have always loved being told what I want to hear, so this sounded good to me. In my heart however, I never felt comfortable taking a synthetic drug. I would later hear differing opinions on HRT from other doctors. If I have learned anything, it's that there is a study and an opinion for everything and they seem to change on a regular basis. Maddening to say the least. I wish I had trusted my instincts more, but life doesn't come with a rewind button.

9 PANDORA'S BOX

As I sat in the waiting room at Dr. Pritchard's office, I officially began the annual freak-out. I said a few Hail Marys and hoped for the best. The technician finally called my name and ushered me into the mammogram room. I never understood why I bothered changing into that flimsy paper cover-up that I immediately removed once the tech came back into the room. I always felt so vulnerable standing there half naked, waiting for this stranger to take my breasts into her hands.

And then the squeeze fest began. She gently placed my breasts on the mammogram machine before pressing down on the cold transparent plate. It always reminded me of a chicken cutlet being flattened under a piece of wax paper, a barbaric process to say the least. The tech took two pictures of each breast with me standing in different positions. When we finished she told me to put the paper gown back on while I waited for the mammogram results from the doctor.

The five minutes until Dr. Pritchard walked in to give me a thumbs up or down always felt like an eternity. This year would be different. When the door opened it was the technician who announced she needed one more picture of my right breast. A red flag! When I asked why, she nonchalantly said it was due to a scar I had on that side, a remnant from a mole I had removed years before. Okay, I bought that. A few minutes later Dr. Pritchard came in and said everything looked fine on my films. Phew! Another bullet dodged.

I always had an ultrasound to be more thorough and hopefully catch anything my mammogram might miss. Fortunately, my insurance paid for it because of my BRCA2 status. That is the only benefit of being a gene carrier. As Dr. Pritchard moved the transducer (a small hand-held device that resembles a microphone attached to the scanner by a cord) over my right breast, I watched him pause and go over the same area several times. And then I heard the words that changed my life.

"I think I see something here."

Instant heart palpitations! He pointed to what looked like a dark, empty area. As he mapped it out on the screen he said it measured approximately 1.4 centimeters. At a time like this, he's using the metric system? Give me a break! My brother would later inform me there are 2.54 centimeters in an inch, which made my lump a little larger than half an inch. It looked like nothing discernible to me; however, I knew in the pit of my stomach it was something.

After getting dressed, I spoke with Dr. Pritchard. He strongly recommended I have a bilateral breast MRI. There was some good news. He was mildly suspicious of a malignancy. "Mildly" sounded much more favorable than "highly" suspicious, but I still felt very weak in the knees.

Better to be safe than sorry and get it checked out. He suggested I go to the Aurora Breast Center at UC Irvine, where they had a dedicated MRI machine for breasts.

The minute I got in the car I dialed Big Al's number at the office. He answered and said, "How did it go, Hon?"

My reply was, "The jig is up!"

What an odd thing to say. I had never used that line before. Crazy to be quoting a line from Annie at a time like this. Being the eternal optimist, my better half assured me it would be nothing. Yeah right! Never believe someone when they say that. It's purely a calming tactic and it failed miserably! I had witnessed too much with my mother and her sisters. Pandora's box was wide open.

I tried to schedule my MRI appointment the minute I got home, but had to wait for precertification from my insurance company. The waiting was the worst part throughout my whole ordeal. Fortunately, I had excellent insurance coverage, which alleviated some of my anxiety. I cannot imagine what it would be like to be uninsured in my shoes.

The first available appointment was for Friday, March 27th: four long, anxiety-filled days away. Breast cancer is so prevalent it is nearly impossible to get right in and get things done. Every three minutes a woman in the U.S. is diagnosed with breast cancer, and every fourteen minutes someone will die of the disease—staggering statistics.

That evening I had dinner with my dear friend Carrie and her college-aged daughter, Amanda. Carrie and I have been friends since our older children were in nursery school. She always has my best interests at heart and is the one I run to when life begins to unravel. I wanted to tell her what was going on; however, she was mired in her own aggravation. Her husband had recently been arrested and charged with fraud. Now more than ever she needed my support and encouragement. There was no way I would impose my stuff on her.

I'm not sure how I got through dinner without dissolving into tears, but I kept it together. I have always appreciated the fragility of life and have been well aware of the fact that everything can change in a moment, but for both of us to be going through traumatic events at the same time was unthinkable. The old adage misery loves company never rang truer. We would cling to each other as we became familiar with our new realities. Words like core biopsy, fraud, divorce and prison were not in our vocabularies. Who would have thought at our age we would be forced to learn a new vernacular?

10 SPIRITUAL CHORD

I convinced Big Al I could take myself to my MRI appointment. As I drove the hour down to Irvine from my home in Sherman Oaks I tried to remain calm. I listened to Jennifer Hudson sing *You Pulled Me Through* all the way down the 405 freeway. It hit a spiritual chord and provided some much needed solace. It would become my anthem over the next several months.

As I got closer to Irvine I reminded myself this could be a false alarm. After all, I had two breast MRIs in recent years. The baseline MRI showed very slight irregularities, but a three-month follow-up done by Dr. Guiliano proved to be normal. That, however, was three years before. I was kicking myself now for not continuing annual MRIs. My friend, Carrie, told me the prior spring the American Cancer Society had changed their screening recommendations for BRCA carriers. They were now recommending an annual breast MRI in addition to mammography. I had promised her I would go and have another one ASAP, but circumstances caused me to postpone. Big Al had been very ill, battling a rare form of pneumonia and subsequently a pulmonary embolism. In the middle of his health woes, his mother died from Chronic Obstructive Pulmonary Disease (COPD). Life kept getting in the way. Cancer, however, doesn't allow anything to get in its way. Lessons learned.

Concerned, I asked my gynecologist if it would be prudent to have another MRI. He had been my doctor for twenty-four years and knew my medical history better than anyone. He is an extraordinary physician with a compassionate bedside manner and follow-up skills I have rarely seen in a doctor. I have always trusted him implicitly. He performed my total hysterectomy and at the time suggested I get rid of everything in one fell swoop, breasts and ovaries, but I thought that was too radical and chose not to remove my breasts. This time I would listen to his recommendation. He made a good case to forego an annual MRI because there were too many false positives being detected, resulting in unnecessary invasive procedures. He believed mammogram along with ultrasound was sufficient in detecting early stage disease.

What was I thinking? So what if I received a false positive? Having an invasive procedure is certainly unpleasant, but what are we talking about here? You get pricked with a needle or have a lumpectomy. The end result with a false positive is the same: no cancer. There is always the possibility of infection with any invasive procedure, but the benefit of early detection outweighs the risk. And a little needle prick or a lumpectomy sure beats a double mastectomy.

The truth is, a mammogram cannot give you a 360-degree picture of the breast. Dense breasts are even more difficult to read. Women leave their mammograms thinking they're in the clear, but it's just one checkpoint, which is why monthly self-breast exams are so imperative along with other diagnostic tools such as ultrasound and MRI when warranted. An early stage breast cancer can take years to show up on a film and some can be felt before they're seen. Although my breasts were average in size, a 34B, they were moderately dense. In hindsight, I believe I may have benefited from having digital mammograms, which my radiologist did not offer. With digital mammography, the magnification, orientation, brightness, and contrast of the image may be altered after the exam to help the radiologist see certain areas more clearly. I can't help examining the steps I missed, but looking in the rear view mirror serves no purpose other than to make one regretful.

11 POKER FACE

All that fretting with my gynecologist about whether or not to have an annual MRI and now I was forced to have one to rule out a malignancy. Believe me, it's always better to have a test as a preventive measure versus a diagnostic procedure.

Upon arrival at the Aurora Breast Center, I once again filled out the requisite forms and waited to be called. A breast MRI is done with the individual lying flat facing downward, with each breast in a cone-shaped device. In a dedicated breast machine both breasts are scanned at the same time. The MRI takes about twenty minutes. The only plus about the deafening knocking sound of the machine is that it drowns out your own dark thoughts. When the test was over I stared at the technician's face for any clues, but she had a poker face. I gained zero information from her, other than to be told my doctor would be getting back to me with the results. Great! More waiting.

Big Al and I were supposed to go skiing over the weekend, but I was paralyzed with anxiety. We cancelled our trip and stayed close to home to wait for any news from the doctor. I'm typically an optimist, but let's face it: no amount of optimism would change the results. In this case I was a realist. So I waited and hoped for the best. As the day wore on I heard nothing. No news is good news, right? Wrong! That's something else people will tell you to keep you calm. No news is simply no news.

I emailed Dr. Pritchard before the day ended to give him a nudge. The thought of waiting until Monday was unbearable. He wrote back and said he had not heard from the radiologist at Aurora and generally no news meant good news. So maybe it was true and I had nothing to worry about.

By late Friday I realized I had left my most prized possession at the breast center. As I glanced down at my left hand I saw my mother's wedding band was missing. I had worn it for thirty-two years, since the day she died, and now it was gone. A sign! Not sure what kind of a sign, but if I were a betting woman I would put money down that bad news was around the corner. I called the breast center and luckily they found Mom's ring. I would pick it up on Monday, along with a CD of my films and the radiologist's report.

The only other time I misplaced my mother's ring was in October 2001, during an Avon Breast Cancer Walk. It was a three-day, sixty-mile walk from Santa Barbara to Malibu. I had never participated in an event like that, but I had come to a point in my life where I felt it was time to get off the sidelines and help. It was a spur of the moment decision, and one of the best ones I have ever made. I signed up to give back, but gained an immeasurable amount in return. My friends and family rallied quickly and helped me raise significant dollars to increase breast cancer awareness.

As a surprise, my family took my favorite white sleeveless T-shirt and had it embroidered in pink. Down one side it read, "Go Mom", and on the other, "POTA", which is our family mantra for Push On Try Again. And on my back was written, "In Memory of My Mother and Her 5 Sisters." I wore it proudly and it remains one of my most prized possessions to this day. It also drew a lot of attention. So many people stopped to ask me about my family and offered comfort and encouragement. It was emotional, yet cathartic and uplifting. For the first time in decades, I did not feel alone. I was surrounded by thousands of women and men with similar stories who were walking for a cure. We were committed to stamping out the disease that had claimed so many lives. We were a band of participants and survivors who were in it to end it.

I had decided to do the Avon Walk alone. I knew I would have six women walking with me in spirit. Big Al drove me to the event and would be there for me at various checkpoints cheering me on and bolstering my spirits. I had some otherworldly moments happen to me along the way, the first as we pulled into our parking space at the registration site. There was an SUV pulling in right next to us, and out jumped a beautiful young girl with long dark hair. As I glanced over, I noticed a tattoo on her arm that read "In Memory of Irene". Alan and I looked at each other, dumbfounded. My mother's American nickname was Irene. I asked the young girl about her tattoo and she said she was walking in memory of her mother. I shared with her that my mother's name had also been Irene. We both took a deep breath. Maybe our mothers were sending us a sign.

A short while later Big Al and I were sitting in the orientation meeting and I saw the same young woman walking down the aisle towards us. I was able to get her attention and inquired, "By the way, I never asked you your name."

She matter-of-factly replied, "It's Nicki."

It's a wonder I didn't pass out right there and then. Instead, all of my apprehensions about doing the walk were washed away. There was no doubt my mother was all around me.

The first day I was fortunate enough to meet four women from Kansas who were repeat offenders, having done the Avon Walk a couple of times before. They walked in support of friends who had battled the disease. They took me under their wing and we talked all day, hardly coming up for air.

I gravitated towards Margie; I felt as if I had known her all my life. The first day was more of a leisurely stroll. We stopped for lunch, refueled and took our time walking the first twenty miles. Big Al was right there at the finish, sharing the exciting news that our daughter, Ally, had been elected vice president of her freshman class in high school. It had been a very good day all around.

The second day began early. I couldn't find my Kansas friends amidst the throngs of women. I must admit I didn't try very hard because there was a part of me that wanted to walk alone. I decided to dedicate that day to my mother and me. I walked as fast as I could, only briefly stopping to pick up some Gatorade and Power Bars.

At one point I met up with two women. We chatted for a bit, until I decided to go full steam ahead. Just as I was leaving them, I inquired about their names. Both of them were Irene. Any doubts I ever had that my mother was watching over me were erased. Even as I write about it, I still cannot believe that happened. I ended up finishing tenth that day out of 3,000 participants, a respectable showing in memory of Bianchina "Irene" Buschi Boscia.

The third day, I easily found my Kansas friends. They were all appropriately dressed as Dorothy from the Wizard of Oz, down to their blue gingham pinafores, and braided pigtail wigs. Talk about attention getters, they stole the show. They proclaimed that I was their Toto for the day. I could not have been more proud to walk beside them. We all wanted to have a good showing so we walked at a brisk pace. One of the women developed painful blisters and had to stop and get bandaged in triage, so one of the other Dorothys stayed with her.

Margie and I, along with her sister-in-law, decided to put the pedal to the metal and bring the walk home as fast as we could. We were flying down Pacific Coast Highway (PCH) when all of a sudden I glanced down and noticed my mother's ring was not on my finger. Of all days not to be wearing it; I felt sick to my stomach. Margie suggested we stop and call the hotel where I stayed the night before to see if housekeeping might have found it. We stood on the side of PCH overlooking the Pacific as I frantically made the call. No luck, the ring had not been found. We regrouped for a second and then decided we had to finish strong. Margie wisely said maybe it was my mother's way of saying it was time to move on and it was okay. I found that comforting in the moment and decided to race ahead.

A short while later, as we came closer to Malibu, we saw a group of lunatic fans jumping up and down, hollering, cheering and waving signs. As we drew nearer, I realized it was my family. My newly crowned vice president of her freshman class, my Ally "cat" was there waving a huge sign and my twelve year old son, Matt, was screaming at the top of his lungs. My sister-in-law Renée was jogging all around us cheering us on, while Big Al and his brother Howard, holding onto his four-month-old son Aaron, looked on with family pride. There are no words to describe the love and support I felt in that moment. The ring didn't matter. It was the people who meant the most. I was blessed with so many beautiful memories of my mother and her sisters. Not even cancer could take that away.

We finished that day in 25th, 26th, and 27th place and although it was not a race, it was symbolic of our personal race to find a cure. Of the sixty miles journeyed, no mile meant more than the half-mile walked at the end with all of the participants. We gathered together and walked in the sand on the shores of Malibu, survivors in pink out in front, the rest of us walking in unison behind them. The skies were covered in gray and there was a mystical feeling in the air as 3,000 women and men completed a trek of a lifetime they would never forget.

That night as I unpacked my things I saw something shiny at the bottom of my cosmetic case. A sigh of relief when I realized it was my mother's ring; a perfect ending to an incredible journey.

That following week I found out I had the BRCA2 gene. There is never a moment's rest from this cunning opponent. But then, a surprise reminder of the Avon Walk arrived in the mail. My Dorothys sent me a beautiful silver key ring, inlaid with a red ruby slipper engraved with the words, "There's no place like home!" The other side read, "Click your heels for a cure." If only it was that simple.

12 NAYSAYERS

Big Al and I spent a quiet weekend at home. We took a long walk at the beach and convinced each other we would stay strong and get through whatever news I received. By Sunday I started feeling more relaxed and began thinking I just might get good news after all.

Big Al went to work Monday morning and I did my usual chores around the house. At 9:30 the phone rang. Caller ID alerted me it was the Beverly Hills Diagnostic Breast Center. Dr. Pritchard was on the other end and the minute I heard the serious tone in his voice I knew the outcome. The MRI confirmed his suspicions. I had a 1.4-centimeter mass in my right breast that was most likely breast cancer. The good news was my lymph nodes looked clear, which meant it was probably a very early stage malignancy. A core biopsy would confirm those results. He asked if I could come in at 12:30 for the test. I felt as if someone had sucked all the air out of my lungs. I thought of my mother and how strong she had been. I would get through this one step at a time.

I called Big Al to come home and drive me to the test. My next call was to my brother. I wanted to get his opinion on my situation. He was puzzled by the need for a core biopsy. It was an invasive procedure that seemed unnecessary considering the fact that I had already decided to have a double mastectomy regardless of the outcome. I was done with the twins no matter what. I told him according to my doctor it was standard protocol used to diagnose the type of breast cancer.

There are naysayers out there who do not believe in core biopsies. They feel strongly the procedure may result in the spreading of cancer cells to nearby lymph nodes. In retrospect, I should not have rushed into that decision. But again, no shoulda, coulda, woulda. I was eager to get a diagnosis and knew I would have the results the next day. As we drove to Dr. Pritchard's office I think Big Al still held out hope that the biopsy would be negative; however, with my family history I felt doomed.

13 USUAL SUSPECTS

I had my core biopsy on Monday, March 30th, one long week since my mammogram. As Big Al and I drove past the majestic palm trees in Beverly Hills it was if I was noticing them for the first time. In an inexplicable way, I felt more alive than I ever had. Maybe this journey would liberate me from a lifetime of fear and waiting for the other shoe to drop.

When we arrived at Dr. Pritchard's office, I was ushered into the exam room for the core biopsy. At first I was lying flat on my back with my feet at the end of the table. Dr. Pritchard began the ultrasound to locate the lump in order to do a guided core biopsy. He was having difficulty finding it so he had me turn around on the table with my head at the end, an awkward position for me. He asked me to roll slightly onto my left side. Once the biopsy point was determined, the skin was prepared with alcohol and anesthetized with Lidocaine. When he zeroed in on the target I heard a loud pop and felt a quick jolt of pressure. I was caught off guard, not having been forewarned regarding the sound and the force of the biopsy. He ended up shooting the needle in two more times in order to get a few different tissue cores for analysis. When it was over, he bandaged me up and called my husband in to tell us next steps. The results would be back the next day and he recommended I begin making appointments with breast surgeons for at least two opinions on how to proceed.

At the top of his list was Dr. Kristi Pado Funk, the former head of Cedars Sinai's Breast Center who had recently opened her own private practice in Beverly Hills. I would also consider the other usual suspects in L.A., including Dr. Armando Guiliano at St. John's and a top breast surgeon at a Los Angeles teaching hospital. I couldn't face Dr. Guiliano after he had recommended years earlier that I have prophylactic mastectomies. He would never have said I told you so, but would be a constant reminder of that glaringly wrong decision. Hindsight is a curse. I also knew in my heart I wanted a female surgeon, someone who would be empathetic and offer encouragement in a way only a woman can.

It was overwhelming for me to even think about the long process I was facing. I just wanted to crawl in bed and pull the covers over my head. I wanted to call Ally and Matt, but decided I would wait to tell them. I did not want to needlessly worry them. Better they should concentrate on their studies and finish the semester strong.

In retrospect, I should have told Ally and Matt immediately. They are young adults and had the maturity to handle the situation. Instead, a week or so later, after much discussion regarding when to tell them, Big Al blurted it out to Ally right before she went on stage for a dance performance. Bad timing! At least she had something to divert her attention. Afterwards, she let him know how annoyed she was at not being told sooner. When she called me, I lost it. She wanted to fly right home to be with me, but I begged her to stay and enjoy the last few weeks of her senior year. She reluctantly complied. I promised her I would be sitting proud as a peacock at her graduation. Nothing would stop me. Matt's a different story. He is my Zen child who takes everything in life in stride, unless of course it's happening to him. When Big Al told him, he expressed concern, but also believed everything would be all right. He called immediately and reassured me I would be fine. I felt relieved.

That night I tossed and turned. My breast was throbbing from the core biopsy and my brain was on overdrive. Tomorrow would be March 31st, eight days since my mammogram. I just wanted to get the show on the road.

The following morning crept by without a word from Dr. Pritchard. Big Al worked from home that day and I puttered around the house for most of the morning. Each hour seemed like an eternity. At 1:30 p.m., as I sat at my desk, my business line rang. It was Dr. Pritchard with my results. It was confirmed. I had invasive ductal cancer, the typical "garden variety" kind that 70% of women with breast cancer have. Dr. Pritchard believed it was early stage and thought I would "do very well." Whatever that meant. He said the cancer began in the ducts and spread outside the walls, making it invasive into the lymphatic system of the breast. The word invasive freaked me out. I thanked him for his time and hung up the phone.

Tears began to fall as I walked into my son's room, where Big Al was busy working at his desk. He was on the phone, looked up and immediately knew from the expression on my face that the results were not what we were hoping for.

I have never felt a more surreal moment in my life than when I said the words, "I have breast cancer." It had been forty-seven years since my mother had been diagnosed. Now it was my turn. Could I muster up her unconquerable spirit? You betcha! All I needed was a plan.

That evening the doorbell rang unexpectedly. My good friend Caryn stopped by with a beautiful bouquet of flowers and some carrot, beet and celery juice. She wanted to ensure I didn't waste a second getting on the healthy bandwagon. I so appreciated her pep talk and fighting spirit.

Caryn is a therapist who knows me like an open book. She is also aware of one of my deep-seated fears: my mother and maternal grandparents all died at the age of fifty-eight. That number has always loomed large for me.

Caryn wrote me an e-mail and said, "Sometimes in life you have to get messed up in order to step up." It was time to reprogram my negative thoughts. Caryn asked me to try on the following positive affirmations for size.

I will begin envisioning a life beyond fifty-eight doing all the things I love to do.

I will begin letting go of past thoughts and focusing on what I want for now and the future.

I will have a second spring filled with grandchildren and a long active life.

I will not be afraid anymore.

I have always been an eternal optimist; however, circumstances had planted weeds in my garden. Being positive is a choice, and it was one I would vow to make every day for the rest of my life.

14 WHO YOU KNOW

The next morning the first call I made was to the only contemporary I knew (at the time) who had breast cancer. She is a longtime client and dear friend. The first thing she said is, "Nicki, this is not a death sentence. I know it feels like blunt force trauma, but you will be okay. Just take it one step at a time and don't get too ahead of yourself."

Kate, in all situations, always says the perfect thing. Unlike other people I know, who said insensitive things like, "If you knew you had the gene why didn't you get rid of them earlier?" or "Do you have a family history?" When I replied "Yes" to the latter question, I could see the sigh of relief. I knew what they were thinking: it couldn't happen to them because it did not run in their family. They clearly didn't know only one in eight women who are diagnosed with breast cancer have a family history. It made my hair stand on end when someone would say, "Well at least in your case it wasn't totally unexpected. This is something you've worried about for years." As if it was a self-fulfilled prophesy and I had somehow willed myself to get breast cancer. Still others intimated that all my repressed grief must have finally come home to roost. That was like rubbing salt in the wound. In my opinion, people look for excuses to make themselves feel better because they have their own underlying fear about getting cancer. Looking for blame or cause serves no purpose. We can only control how we react to a situation and how we grow from the experience. Hopefully, it makes us more resilient and empathic human beings.

The bottom line is, in life, shit happens for a variety of reasons, to everyone. It does not discriminate and eventually we all pay the piper. When I told Kate what people were saying she didn't skip a beat.

"People say stupid things, ignore them."

And that's exactly what I did.

There were times I felt I was in a Curb Your Enthusiasm episode. People actually hinted I had the "good" kind of cancer. Breast cancer survival is so prevalent that some people do not consider it to be as serious as other malignancies. They must not realize that approximately 40,000 women and 400 men a year in the U.S. will die from the disease. Believe me, there is nothing good about any kind of cancer. It all sucks.

Cancer has a way of highlighting the true colors of the people in your life. Some will run and hide out of fear. Others will go overboard with inappropriate attention and advice. Surprisingly, some of the people closest to me disappointed me the most. Maybe they were scared and could not fathom the idea I might be ill, because I was their rock. I choose to believe that they cared deeply, and were just struggling with their own feelings about this life-changing event. Nonetheless, there would be friendship casualties along the way.

The truth is, I did not want to be smothered with a lot of attention. I have always enjoyed my privacy and solitude. I craved normalcy and responded best to email and texts. I did not want to repeat the same story over and over again and give daily updates regarding the latest doctor's appointment, test results or scale of pain from one to ten. It was draining for Big Al and me and we needed to keep up our strength.

Word to the wise: if you really want to help out a friend who is ill, drop off a healthy dinner at the doorstep. Don't ring the bell, just leave it with a nice note. My neighbor and dear friend Marylou, who lives across the street, was right on the money. She would bring me a cup of green tea every morning without expecting conversation. Her husband, Jeff, would cook dinner and leave it at the door, calling ahead to let us know he was dropping it off.

My sweet friend Cheryl bent over backwards, driving me to doctor appointments, cooking meals and lending an ear when I needed someone to listen. At one point someone remarked Cheryl could do more because she didn't work. I was not keeping score among my friends and this was no time for a competition. Cheryl did more because she was on a personal mission to nurse me back to health. I will never be able to find the words to thank her for lifting me up when I sunk to the bottom of the abyss.

I understood everyone was doing the best they could and I had the deepest appreciation for all of the encouragement and support I received. I was especially touched when my long time friend Jimmy Boy Sullivan sent me the book <u>Traveling Mercies</u> by Anne Lamott. It took me a while to pick it up and read it, but once I did I could not put it down. I began researching Anne Lamott and discovered something she said about grace in an Amazon interview regarding another one of her books, <u>Grace (Eventually): Thoughts on Faith</u>. It summed up my emotions perfectly.

> *"Grace is not something I do, or can chase down: but it is something I can receive, when I stop trying to be in charge. We communicate grace to one another by holding space for people when they are hurt or terrified instead of trying to fix them, or manage their emotions for them. We offer ourselves as silent companionship, or gentle listening when someone feels alone. We get glasses of water when they are thirsty."*

I could not have said it better myself. No one could fix me or manage my emotions. I just needed time. It was enough to know that people cared and were there for me if I needed them.

When I was anxiety-ridden I reached out to my cherished confidante Susan. There was more than one occasion when she talked me off the ledge. She knew my reaction to my diagnosis had more to do with the sad memories from my childhood than the situation at hand. Susan had a way of compartmentalizing things and making me take a deep breath. She also stocked my freezer with quarts of homemade chicken soup that was so comforting during those dark days.

My pragmatic friend Carla called me every morning to check in and make sure I was okay. She had thyroid cancer years before I met her. I have known her since our older children were in the third grade. Five years ago she was diagnosed with melanoma. I remember the day she called and nonchalantly said, "We have a situation over here," as if a pipe had just burst in her kitchen.

When she blurted out, "I have melanoma," I felt sick to my stomach, but kept my reaction in check so as not to upset her. Carla takes all things in life in stride, including cancer. She is the perfect example of someone who had cancer, but cancer never had *her*. She had a huge impact on the way I approached my own "situation".

15 MONDAY MORNING QUARTERBACK

Kate had consulted with one breast surgeon, the top doctor from the Los Angeles teaching hospital I referenced before, and loved her. She did not get a second opinion. Kate, unlike me, does not analyze things to death. She is a decisive woman who trusts her instincts. I, on the other hand, beat a dead horse until it disintegrates. One opinion would never suffice for me. I suffer from analysis paralysis. Kate highly recommended her surgeon, but was concerned I would not be able to get in to see her right away.

Big Al called a dear friend and physician at the teaching hospital who immediately facilitated a meeting with the surgeon. It's almost unheard of to get in to see a top doctor so quickly. In life, it's all about whom you know, a frustrating fact unless you have connections that can deliver.

I had an appointment the following day, April 1st, at 4:30 p.m.—nine long days since my mammogram. April Fool's Day, but nobody was fooling anyone here. I was also able to schedule a meeting with Dr. Funk for Thursday morning, April 2nd. Besides my radiologist, two close friends had recommended her. I began feeling empowered, knowing I might have a plan by the end of the week.

Prior to meeting with the surgeon, I raced down to Irvine to pick up the CD of my MRI along with the radiologist's report, and my mother's ring.

It was back on my finger and I felt instantly protected. I also had to swing by Beverly Hills to get my mammograms from the past three years from Dr. Pritchard. I saw him briefly when I was there. He reassured me he thought I would do well and his kindness brought a tear to my eye. I have always been a sucker for a gentle touch.

Visiting the cancer center at the teaching hospital was a stressful experience. As I walked into the below-ground facility I was overcome by a wave of claustrophobia. Right or wrong, environment is key to me. I did not like being in a hospital setting with a labyrinth of buildings and hallways. As my gynecologist wisely said, there is no need to be in a teaching facility for early stage breast cancer. I should have listened to him; however, I had to investigate things for myself.

I knew instantly I was in the wrong place, but I sat down, filled out forms (again) and waited my turn. For the next several months this would be my life: doctor's appointments, surgeries and adjuvant therapy to treat my cancer. Even now I can hardly say the word. My mother and her sisters referred to it as the "Big C". It was all so hush-hush back then. Today breast cancer is a household topic and a lucrative business. Every time I turn around there seems to be another advertisement for an Avon walk, a Revlon run, a Mt. Shasta climb or a Susan G. Komen fundraiser, amongst countless other events. Pink ribbons abound and the month of

October is dedicated to National Breast Cancer Awareness. Countless money has been raised, but still, we have no cure.

The surgeon called us into the exam room and reviewed my history. She examined my breasts and closely studied my mammograms from 2007, 2008 and 2009. She was soft-spoken, direct, and unintentionally scared the hell out of me. Looking at my films she pointed to something as far back as 2007 on my mammogram. She admitted it is always easier to find something when you know where to look. I have never appreciated Monday morning quarterbacks because they only serve as a pointless reminder of what you could have done differently after it's too late. She also mentioned my tumor might be as large as two centimeters, which would change the staging, but she wouldn't know for certain until she operated.

How could my cancer be any greater than Stage I? I watched myself like a hawk; I did everything my doctors told me to do, shy of having the mastectomies. How could my cancer grow so large from one year to the next? She told me the cancer could have been there for as long as eight years, but with dense breasts like mine it was difficult to detect. WTF? All those years of radiation from mammograms for what? And what about all the ultrasounds and MRIs? I was exasperated to say the least.

I didn't know what specific kind of invasive ductal cancer I had, other than it was moderately differentiated—meaning the cancer cells appear moderately different from surrounding, normal tissue—, because Dr. Pritchard had not ordered a comprehensive biopsy. I was still in the dark as to whether the tumor was estrogen positive or negative and HER2 positive or negative, results that would determine how aggressive my cancer was and the recommended course of treatment.

Additionally, the surgeon was concerned because it looked as though the tumor was close to the chest wall. OMG! This was a lot to take in and I had no clue what it all meant. I could not wait to get home and Google up a storm, a very dangerous thing to do. My advice, step away from the computer unless you're consulting WebMD. Too many rogue sites on the internet give misinformation. You could diagnose yourself to death!

She recommended I have a double mastectomy since I had a 50% chance of getting cancer in my other breast because of the BRCA2 gene. She also said I should immediately stop taking hormones and seemed surprised I had been taking them for as long as I had with my BRCA2 status. I knew it! I should never have been on HRT, let alone for eighteen years. I had to snap out of it and stop regretting my decisions. What was done was done. The fact was, the estrogen did not cause my cancer, but, I would later find out it fueled it.

We discussed potential dates for surgery and she recommended a couple of plastic surgeons practicing at the teaching hospital for reconstruction, which would begin at the same time as the mastectomies. That's when I would learn the so-called best plastic surgeons in L.A. want their entire 'do re mi' up front.

Unbelievable! I can just imagine what my clients would say if I told them I wanted to be paid in full at the start of an engagement. They would tell me to go pound sand. But we were talking about my ta-tas here and I wanted the best. My insurance company would agree to cover 60%. That's a whole lot of out-of-pocket change; somewhere in the neighborhood of ten grand by the time I was done. I was very fortunate to be able to afford that kind of expense.

Ally would be graduating May 16th, so I wanted to have my surgery as soon as possible in order to have enough time to recuperate prior to flying back East for the big day. The surgeon said there was no need to rush. Easy for her to say. She wasn't the one with cancer lurking in her body. She suggested I have a lumpectomy prior to graduation and have the mastectomies in June. No way I wanted to have two procedures and undergo general anesthesia twice. The real issue seemed to be her calendar and coordinating dates with a plastic surgeon.

Big Al and I were so shell-shocked and overwhelmed with information that we left my records with the surgeon and gave her the impression she would be performing my surgery. We walked to the car dejected. We were exhausted and needed to regroup.

My cell phone began ringing off the hook with texts and calls. Concerned friends wanted to know the latest, but I was too drained to speak to anyone except for Carrie, the voice of reason in the middle of a shit storm. She advised me to take a deep breath, keep my appointment with Dr. Funk and go meet with her for a second opinion. Carrie works in the medical field and highly recommended Dr. Funk. She was certain Dr. Funk would be the perfect fit. Besides being a gifted surgeon, Dr. Funk had recently left Cedars-Sinai and had just moved to a suite of offices in a Beverly Hills medical building. I believe it is important to feel encouraged and uplifted by your doctor and the environment in which you will be treated. The last thing you want is to feel uncomfortable and scared. How can you fight if you're feeling deflated and frightened?

When I got home I immediately got into bed and sobbed for hours. I could not stop thinking about my mother and her sisters and how they managed to get through this at a time when there were few treatment options and they had young children to raise. You never know what someone is going through until you walk in his or her shoes.

Big Al and I had to race back to the teaching hospital early the next morning on our way to Dr. Funk's office to get all of my records. A word of advice: never leave your records behind. Treat them as if they were your children and don't let them out of your sight.

16 PINK LOTUS

Dr. Funk had opened her new offices on Spalding Drive in Beverly Hills on March 23rd, the day of my mammogram. What kind of timing is that? Looking back, our lives were clearly meant to intersect.

Dr. Funk's offices were still under construction when we met with her on the morning of April 2nd. I loved the fact that the newly named Pink Lotus Breast Center was not in a hospital setting. I sat in one of the few chairs in the waiting room and filled out forms again. Why isn't there a universal medical form to save patients a lot of time and hassle?

Still feeling dejected by the preceding day's events, I was skeptical this would be worth my time. I was growing impatient when the nurse practitioner finally called my name. She led us to an exam room where she asked me to change into a white cloth robe. What a nice departure from the paper cover-ups you're given at most doctor's offices, the ones that barely fit and you're never sure if the opening goes in the front or back. It felt very comfortable and dignified.

From the minute Dr. Funk walked into the room I knew she was the one. She is brilliant, calm and incredibly kind, with the hands of a gifted surgeon. Did I mention she is beautiful too? At the time she was pregnant with triplet boys. Anyone else would have been on bed rest, but instead she had just started a new venture. She told me her last day in the office would be May 14th. I later found out she worked up until early July, right before her boys were born.

Kristi Funk is one of those people who can do it all seamlessly. Her undergraduate degree in psychology from Stanford is evident in the way she interacts with people. Her compassion fills the room and in an instant she slays the doom and gloom in the air.

She took a moment to look at my records and noticed I did not have a comprehensive report of my tumor type. She asked me to pick up the block slides from Dr. Pritchard in order to send them out for further analysis. She was hoping my cancer was estrogen positive, and HER2 negative, a less aggressive form of the disease which studies showed responded well to an aromatase inhibitor like Tamoxifen. Size of the tumor and staging would determine the need for chemo. Like the teaching hospital surgeon, she recommended I undergo a double mastectomy because of the BRCA2 gene.

When I told her I was concerned about the size of my tumor and lymph node involvement, she said, "Let's take a look."

As she glided the ultrasound transducer over my right breast and underarm she proclaimed, "You have a very boring armpit. Your lymph nodes look clear and don't even show any of the typical swelling from a core biopsy."

She said the lump was approximately 1.35 x .82 centimeters, and she did not seem to think she would find anything different when she operated.

I also mentioned a lump I had in my neck for decades that the surgeon whom I'd already seen had expressed concern about.

She said, "Let's take a look at that too," and quickly added, "It's nothing!"

What a relief! I would not have to wait for the results of an unnecessary PET scan.

She handed me some information on the options for the management of breast cancer, including one that outlined my risk factor. With each passing year beginning at age thirty my chances of getting breast cancer increased. At age fifty-two I had a 34% chance of getting the disease, maxing out at age eighty with an 85% risk factor. I would later tell my gynecologist that I felt those odds were still in my favor. It was just luck of the draw and I came up shorthanded. He drew a chilling analogy to put it in perspective for me. He said, "If you knew your daughter had a 34% chance of getting raped when she left the house, would you let her out the door?" My answer was a resounding, "No!" But it was too late to press the reset button.

At least at that point it appeared as though my cancer was Stage 1, less than two centimeters without lymph node involvement. Dr. Funk mentioned that radiation would only be required if I had any of the following: more than four positive lymph nodes, a tumor greater than five centimeters, extensive lymphatic/vessel invasion or close margins. Everything would be determined by the final pathology report. Little did I know that I would not have the final test results for another eight weeks. An eternity, and what a roller coaster ride it would be!

In the meantime, I told her I would be continuing acupuncture as well as cranial sacral treatments with my chiropractor. In the lobby I had noticed she offered acupuncture within her practice. When I asked her who the resident acupuncturist was, she replied, "Dr. Mao from the Tao of Wellness." Talk about signs: Dr. Mao had been treating me for years for my MS. It was reassuring to know she embraced eastern medicine and it felt good to know we were on the same page.

As luck would have it, Dr. Funk had a cancellation for April 14th and could perform the surgery at Cedars-Sinai as long as I could line up a plastic surgeon. That would give me enough time to recuperate prior to Ally's graduation, which was my main concern. My mother had passed away the year before I graduated from Franklin & Marshall College. I had to be there for my girl.

Dr. Funk explained she would perform the bilateral mastectomy with a sentinel node biopsy to make sure the cancer had not spread to nearby lymph nodes. I would know the results of that biopsy when I woke up from surgery. If the cancer had spread to any of the three nodes, she would have to remove additional nodes to send out for further analysis. Based on the ultrasound and MRI, she did not anticipate the cancer had spread.

Dr. Funk recommended two plastic surgeons, including Jay Orringer, with whom she had recently begun working, and R. Kendrick Slate, a plastic surgeon on staff at Cedars. A phone call to Dr. Orringer's office resulted in an appointment later that day. Things were looking up.

17 THE HAPPIEST PLACE ON EARTH

Just when I thought I could not possibly go to another doctor's office and fill out forms, I found myself in the happiest place on earth. At 2:00 p.m. on April 2nd I met an incredible doctor and an extraordinary man. Dr. Jay Orringer would change the direction of my psyche and add some much needed levity to a shitty situation. He would also put me back together and make me whole again.

I went to meet Dr. Orringer alone. I felt the need to discuss my new set of twins in private. I also knew Big Al needed a break from all the madness. Dr. Orringer had worked with Dr. Guiliano for seventeen years, operating out of St. John's Hospital in Santa Monica. He had recently been given operating privileges at Cedars–Sinai Hospital and had worked with Dr. Funk on two cases. Again, perfect timing for me! Cedars-Sinai was my hospital of choice. It's where I had my babies and I felt comfortable there.

Ana Marie, Doctor Orringer's dynamo office manager for the past seventeen years, greeted me. It says a lot about a doctor when they have the same staff for as many years as they have been in practice. Such was the case with Dr. Orringer.

His suite is in the penthouse of a Beverly Hills office building. It felt spa-like and was exactly what I needed. I knew I would be seeing the plastic surgeon for the next year and wanted to be in a place where I felt comfortable. Going to a hospital setting was out of the question. Most importantly, Dr. Orringer was a true mensch. Unlike the other plastic surgeons who had been recommended to me, he did not require full payment up front. Fifty percent of each procedure was collected at the time they were performed. He was willing to wait months for the balance of the money, since plastic surgeons are the last ones to get paid by insurance companies.

Dr. Orringer came out to greet me and shook my hand with both of his, leading me into his office with tender loving care. We sat and talked for two hours. He explained in detail what would happen the day of the surgery. Dr. Funk would remove my breasts and he would immediately begin reconstruction. I would not be leaving the hospital as my mother did, disfigured and unrecognizable. He showed me pictures of his work, the before and after, that were stunning. He was clearly a gifted surgeon and a true artist who cared deeply about his patients and felt it was a privilege to be their physician.

There was no need for a second opinion. I had found my team. Dr. Funk would be my breast surgeon and Dr. Orringer would be my plastic surgeon. I called Dr. Funk's office to give them the go ahead. My bilateral mastectomy was scheduled for April 14th, 7:00 a.m. at Cedars-

Sinai Hospital. I would have to keep myself busy over the next ten days, which felt like a lifetime away.

In order to get prepared for my surgery I began seeing my acupuncturist and chiropractor more frequently. They would help get my body and mind stronger for the long road ahead. I also began taking a 1000 mg. of Vitamin C to aid in the healing process after surgery in addition to Chinese herbs to boost the immune system prescribed by Dr. Mao. Taking a holistic view to my health empowered me. Everything seemed so surreal, like I was watching my life play out on a movie screen. Dark thoughts consumed me at night, but during the day I was able to keep them at bay by staying busy.

As timing would have it, Durlester Consulting, my executive search business, had come to a screeching halt because of the economic downturn. I had been a headhunter for most of my career, specializing in placing professionals in the wealth management field. My diagnosis could not have come at a better time in terms of my professional life. I could concentrate on getting well and would have Big Al to take care of me. Believe me, I realized how fortunate I was to have that kind of financial and emotional support. I was hugely blessed.

As April 14th drew closer, I found myself getting scared about the surgery. There is always the fear that you might not wake up when undergoing general anesthesia, but today those fears are largely unfounded. The waiting was driving me insane.

Two days before my surgery I received great news from Dr. Funk. My comprehensive core biopsy results showed my cancer was estrogen positive, HER2 negative, which meant I had a less aggressive form of breast cancer that could be treated with an aromatase inhibitor, an anti-estrogen drug, after surgery. My final post surgery pathology would determine any additional treatment including chemotherapy and radiation. Receiving that news changed my whole attitude going into surgery. I was uplifted and ready for battle.

18 UPTOWN GIRL

The night before my double mastectomy is a bit of a blur. I remember being in a meditative kind of state. I was trying to keep myself calm without the use of drugs. I had Xanax on hand, but I was able to keep my anxiety in check. Big Al didn't talk much that night. There really weren't any words that would have made me feel better. This was something that I was going to do alone and I needed to get in the zone.

I prayed for strength and courage and thought a lot about my mother. If she could do it, so could I. Strangely enough, I had a very peaceful night's sleep. I awakened at 4:30 a.m. to shower and take one last look at the breasts that had served me well for fifty-two years. Gravity had taken hold years before, after breast-feeding both of my babies. They certainly weren't the perky set they once were. Well, maybe they never were that perky, but they were there and they were mine. I should have appreciated them more and feared them less. I used to joke I hadn't seen myself in my birthday suit in years, being careful to put my contact lenses on *after* I dressed. Being blind as a bat allowed me to protect my image of myself as a young woman.

I remember telling Dr. Funk I was an "uptown girl". To me there was nothing like having Big Al cop a feel. I would not have that kind of stimulation again. My reconstructed breasts would be numb for a long time and I would never have any feeling in my new nipples. They would be crafted from nearby skin, devoid of any nerve endings leading to sexual arousal. A small price to pay for renewed health and longevity.

As I dressed I thought of my children, rushing to their classes at school, probably thinking of their mama bear and concerned about my surgery. I hoped they weren't too worried, because I knew in my heart of hearts I was going to be okay.

I wore my favorite pair of jeans with a black t-shirt to the hospital. I thought about my mother, who never wore pants, let alone jeans, a day in her life. She would have been mortified that I wasn't more appropriately dressed for the occasion. Funny the things you think about in those moments.

While packing, I made sure to include an angel my friend Kate had given me. It would remain by my bedside at the hospital, and is still on my night table at home. I tossed in a zip-up sweatshirt for comfort on the ride home. I would be wearing button-down tops and jackets with zippers for several weeks to come. It would be a while until it felt comfortable to raise my arms up to don a t-shirt or sweater. I also packed a beautiful, pink flowered scarf a dear friend had given me some weeks before, not knowing I would chose to wear that home after my surgery. It would mask my flat chest and give me some dignity as I left the hospital.

Big Al and I left for Cedars-Sinai around 5:30 in the morning. It was still dark outside, but we could hear the early morning hum of the nearby 405 freeway. As the sun began rising over the eastern sky, I remember thinking that life never skips a beat for anyone. I suppose that's the way it should be; otherwise, there would be no rhythm to our lives. April 14th, 2009 may have begun like any other day, but it would clearly be life altering for me.

I began feeling anxious as we pulled into the hospital parking lot. Big Al assured me everything would be fine. I would wake up from surgery and the bogeyman who had been under my bed since I was five years old would finally be gone. I could move on with my life, without the breasts that had caused me so much worry through the years. It would turn out to be a blessing in disguise. That blessing in disguise line always seems to work, although in that moment nothing could make me feel better.

I checked in at the admissions desk, smiling nervously at the administrator. She filled out the necessary forms for me to sign, including the scary one that tells you all the potential risks—including death. She placed a hospital band on my left wrist and asked me to be seated until they called my name. There were so many thoughts flashing through my head, including the lingering fear of anesthesia. What if I didn't wake up from the surgery? Now that would be a big drag for everyone in my life, but I guess for me I wouldn't know the difference. Crazy thoughts!

They called my name and another woman's and we accompanied each other with our husbands on the elevator, making some light conversation to fill the air. We got off on the eighth floor and before I realized it I was being whisked away for surgery, barely having a private moment with Big Al before leaving him. We walked down a long hallway before turning right into pre-op. I looked back to see if Big Al's eyes were following me and he was busy talking on the phone. I couldn't believe it. I had to get his attention for a final thumbs-up. I shouted his name, he looked up and I waved both hands as big as I could. Thank God he saw me and waved back. I felt connected and reassured. From there on out I was on my own.

19 GREY'S ANATOMY

As I walked into the pre-op area a very young and pretty nurse greeted me. I wish I could remember her name. I swore I would never forget it, because she was extraordinarily kind. She told me to fully undress and put on a hospital gown tied in the back. She covered me with warm blankets while I waited for my general surgeon, plastic surgeon and anesthesiologist to arrive. She asked me a series of questions, none of which I can recall. I was too busy watching all the doctors and nurses swarm around. Everything was so surreal. I felt like I was in an episode of Grey's Anatomy. This could not possibly be happening to me. And then, in the midst of all those hospital scrubs, I saw Dr. Orringer, dressed in a suit and carrying his black bag. I was so relieved and happy to see him. I knew I was in good hands.

Dr. Orringer measured me again, to make sure he created a symmetrical set of breasts. He would be implanting expanders and would pump them up with saline to a small A cup. Over the next couple of months, he would continue inflating them with saline until they expanded to my desired size, eventually replacing them with saline or silicone implants. He drew some markings on my breasts and told me I was good to go. Dr. Orringer went to change into his scrubs and would see me in the operating room.

You would think a woman would lose all dignity in this process with everyone examining you and taking a look see, however, it's all done in a dignified, respectful manner. Never a humiliating moment, which is incredible considering how modest I am. I only balked at taking before and after pictures. I've never been one to pose in front of the camera and to have to do it without clothes was mortifying. It did, however, give me an appreciation for the metamorphosis I was undergoing.

Dr. Funk came in next, looking as beautiful and pregnant as ever. I still can't believe she was so close to having triplets. The woman is truly amazing. She was very reassuring and confident the surgery would go well. The only newbie in the process was the anesthesiologist. Some anesthesiologists will call the night before surgery to introduce themselves and find out if you have any questions. I didn't hear a word from mine, which was troublesome for me. He was, after all, the person responsible for keeping me breathing and alive. He turned out to be a very pleasant fellow. One minute he was introducing himself and starting the IV and the next thing I remember is waking up in recovery six and a half hours later. I have no recollection of being wheeled into the operating room and prepped for surgery and I'm glad I don't.

When I first opened my eyes in recovery I saw Dr. Orringer walking around my bed. I have a vague memory of him blurting out that they found cancer in one node. What was he saying? Before I could muster up the strength to ask any questions, he was gone. The recovery nurse on duty said he was calling my husband to come in to see me. When Big Al walked in he had a dejected look on his face. I immediately asked if I had heard Dr. Orringer correctly. "Did they find cancer in one node?"

Big Al nodded his head yes and said, "I'm sorry, honey."

I was devastated and angry, even in my hazy state. I was afraid the one positive node would advance the staging of my cancer and change the recommended treatment plan. It was later confirmed by my oncologist that my breast cancer was now classified as Stage IIA. How could this be? The tumor was so small and nothing had shown up in the nodes on the MRI and ultrasound. I was inconsolable, and then I fell asleep.

I was in and out of consciousness for the next several hours. I had a self-administered morphine pump, which could be pushed every eight minutes. I don't think I ever took my finger off that button. I would be in recovery for several hours since they did not have a room ready for me. Big Al was only allowed to stay with me for a few minutes at a time. My friend, Caryn, came to the hospital to keep him company. I'm glad she did because she made sure he ate and drank during that very long day. I refused to see her because I needed time to digest my new reality.

My throat was incredibly dry and I recall asking for ice chips. I had a hoarse voice from the breathing tube they had inserted during surgery. I kept clearing my throat hoping for some relief. I had a male recovery nurse who was very kind and attentive. I know he felt terrible I had to stay there so long. Finally, around 9:00 p.m. a room became available. It felt so good to move into my own private space. Fortunately, they gave me a large corner room on the eighth floor with beautiful views of the Hollywood Hills. They brought in a cot so Big Al could spend the night. At that point I don't recall having any pain. I was so out of it. My plastic surgeon said I would wake up and feel as though a baby elephant was sitting on my chest and might find it uncomfortable to breathe. It wasn't as bad as I had expected.

After I was moved into the room, a lovely nurse came in to introduce herself. She said her name was Frances and she would be taking care of me through the night. Big Al looked at me in shock with tears in his eyes. His mother's name was Frances. She had passed away the preceding June. We both knew in that moment she was right there with us, watching over me. It was very comforting. So was the magnificent plant I had found waiting for me in the room.

How did anyone know where I was? In true sleuth-like form, my dear friends Kathy and Jay called on their mother, who worked as a volunteer at Cedars, to track me down. For some unknown reason I was listed as a confidential guest. That did not stop Natalie from finding me. She went straight to security and did not give up until she secured my room number. Now that's some detective work and it made my night.

Big Al seemed completely overwhelmed. It's never easy for the caretaker. I know he was relieved the surgery was over, but concerned about the positive node. That would definitely change the course we were on, but we both knew we could get through anything together. I think he had a much more restless night than I. He was talking, laughing and passing gas in his sleep and put on quite a show for the night nurse. What is it with men? Flatulence follows them wherever they go. Finally, at 6:00 a.m., he went home to take a shower and get a couple hours rest.

20 STARBUCKS

As the early morning hours passed I became eager to get up and at least sit in a chair. I wanted to start walking and regaining my strength. I kept drinking as much water as I could to flush out my system and get rid of the aftereffects of general anesthesia. I had a catheter so I didn't have to worry about getting up and going to the bathroom. It would not be easy maneuvering around with all that equipment, including the IV and antibiotic drips.

Later that morning the nurses finally helped me up, sat me in a chair and brought me a liquid breakfast. I did not have much of an appetite, but knew I had to force myself to eat to get my system going.

Dr. Funk came by on her morning rounds to tell me the surgery had gone well, but unfortunately had revealed cancer in the sentinel node. As a result, she removed thirteen additional lymph nodes to be biopsied. The other two nodes she removed on the table were clear, which was a good sign. The final results would be back by Friday, April 17th. She also sent a fresh tissue sample to the Netherlands for a MammaPrint, which would determine my risk for recurrence.

A MammaPrint is an FDA-cleared gene expression profile test validated in node-negative patients to assess an individual's risk of breast cancer recurrence. The test analyzes the seventy critical genes that influence breast tumor progression and the potential for metastasis. In the clinical setting, this translates into reducing unnecessary chemotherapy for women at a low risk of metastasis, while at the same time helping to identify high-risk women who may benefit from therapy.

A "Low Risk" MammaPrint result means a patient has a 10% chance her cancer will recur within ten years without any additional adjuvant treatment, either hormonal therapy or chemotherapy. A "High Risk" MammaPrint result means a patient has a 29% chance that her cancer will recur in ten years without adjuvant treatment. That all sounded well and good, but I was node positive, so how would it help me? I would find out later how important that test was. I began crying and recall Dr. Funk saying I got one free node and hopefully the rest would be negative. To this day, I'm not sure exactly what she meant by that, but it gave me hope and helped me to focus on recovering from surgery.

Big Al looked refreshed when he returned to the hospital. He stopped by Starbucks to bring me my favorite iced green tea. Nothing ever tasted so good. By then Dr. Funk had left and I was back in bed resting. The next time I opened my eyes I saw the most beautiful flower arrangement sitting on the table next to my bed, sent by dear friends from Columbus, Ohio. It was so typical of Jonathan, Leslie and Abbe to have something delivered so quickly. Jonathan and I met while working at Bankers Trust in Manhattan. Our enduring friendship has spanned three decades, including all the ups and downs of our lives. Each year we note the day we met, July 14, 1980, as a reminder of how lucky we are to be best friends. It meant the world to me to know that I was in his family's thoughts and prayers.

By that afternoon my room looked like a flower shop. I have always been the one to say don't spend money on flowers, make a donation instead, but not this time. Being surrounded by all those lovely arrangements lifted my spirits.

My next visitor was Dr. Orringer, who came by to see how I was doing. While he was there the nurses got me back up for another few minutes in the chair. Big Al and Dr. Orringer were sitting at the table in my room discussing the stock market and the current economic downturn when suddenly I felt a searing sensation in my right breast. I couldn't even breathe through it, nor could I get their attention. Unbelievable! I'm ready to pass out and they're oblivious. Thank God the nurse came by and could see I was in pain. She gave me an extra shot of meds, which took the edge off almost immediately. She also directed me to slowly remove the catheter. The very thought made me cringe, however, it turned out to be a no brainer.

Drinking all those fluids, however, caught up to me. The first time I shuffled to the restroom was a wee bit challenging, maneuvering the IV only to find myself facing the mirror. I wanted to take a look at my chest, but wasn't quite ready to see my new reality. I expected to be fully bandaged, but Dr. Orringer had applied two simple pieces of tape covering my stitches, which ran vertically down the lower half of each breast.

I also had four drains under my arms to take care of any fluid build-up. The nurse would train me how to empty them myself. I have always been a squeamish person, however, it wasn't as disgusting as I thought it would be. I had to be careful not to develop lymphedema, an accumulation of excess fluid that can cause severe swelling, due to the removal of the lymph nodes under my right arm. I was advised to not do any heavy lifting, to avoid carrying a heavy purse on my right shoulder, to make sure no one took my blood pressure on that side or used that arm for blood withdrawal. For the first few weeks I was also advised to keep my right arm elevated whenever I was lying down. So much to remember.

21 THELMA AND LOUISE

My third visitor was my brother-in-law, Howard. He is Big Al's younger brother, best friend, and business partner. I agreed to let him visit to keep Big Al company. I had zero interest in seeing anyone and sure as hell did not want anyone to see me. Howard brought my favorite chocolates, See's Candies Nuts and Chews, which was a very sweet gesture, but the last thing I felt like doing was eating. I suppose that reflects my mood at the time, because any other day I would have devoured that whole box.

My new healthy way of eating, however, did not include sugar, or as I like to refer to it, death crystals. I should have given it up years before. I have always been a healthy eater, but now I would become much stricter with my food regimen, including lots of organic fruits, vegetables, whole grains and a diet low in fat and dairy. I hadn't eaten red meat in twenty years since my father's death from colon cancer. Now I would eat more fish, less fowl and would consume foods rich in antioxidants. The only chocolate I would indulge in would be a small piece of dark chocolate to satisfy my sweet tooth. It would not be easy giving up my favorite comfort food. Nothing like a fresh baked chocolate chip cookie or some well-done French fries, not to mention a hot slice of pizza or frozen yogurt. Those foods were now ancient history.

By my second night in the hospital I could see Big Al was exhausted. He was useless so I sent him home around midnight to get a good night's sleep. I would be going home in the morning and needed him rested. I must say I was disappointed he left. I had hoped he could muster up the strength to stay with me. I did not want to be alone.

When Big Al left I texted Marylou. I told her about the one positive node and how scared shitless I was. I still could not fathom my cancer had spread so quickly from one year to the next. She texted me back and forth for what seemed like an hour or so, knowing I needed her company. And then she called and we talked for hours. I will never forget her kindness. She got me through that night. She is the Louise to my Thelma.

The morning I left the hospital I decided to take a sponge bath, which meant finally taking a look at the new twins. The nurse walked me into the bathroom and closed the door to give me a minute alone. I slowly pulled off my hospital gown, looked in the mirror and saw two small, nippleless mounds. I hadn't been this flat-chested since I was twelve. The surgical tape camouflaged the stitches and took up the area where the areola and nipple used to be. Not that bad, just different. Once I put my clothes on, I looked okay. Another hurdle crossed!

22 HOME

Coming home was amazing. In the words of Jane Austen, "There is nothing like staying home for real comfort." Of course every speed bump and pothole along the way sent shock waves of pain shooting through my chest. At least the worst, or so I thought, was behind me. My focus would now be on getting strong enough to attend Ally's graduation. Nothing would keep me from seeing her walk across that stage.

The minute I got home, I changed into some cozy button-down pajamas. Still heavily drugged, I was taking a cocktail of Ativan and Percocet. There was no way I wanted to be put in the position of chasing the pain. I would heal more quickly if I could keep myself pain-free and calm. Friends came by to visit and although their intentions were good, I found it very difficult to entertain an audience.

On Friday, my Italian friend Mary stopped by with Big Al's favorite, homemade Eggplant Parmesan. She sat down on the couch with me to visit for a while. The phone rang and it was Dr. Funk with my biopsy results. I could tell by the look on Big Al's face it was great news. The rest of my nodes were clear. We would have the results of the MammaPrint within ten days or so. I was so glad Mary was there to hear the good news with us. Nothing like being with a *paisan*. Things were looking up again.

On Saturday, two days after I got out of the hospital, I had a houseful of guests. I can hardly remember that day. My friends still remind me I was completely out of it. I think I may have flashed my new set of twins more than once. I knew everyone had a morbid curiosity so why not address the big elephant in the room?

In the midst of all the visitors, Dr. Orringer unexpectedly showed up. Yes, he makes house calls. Unbelievable in this day and age! He came by several times to check on me and remove my drains, and called daily to make sure I was okay. I felt exponentially better once the drains were out. I could finally take a shower. Ah! The simple things gave me so much pleasure.

Nine days after surgery, on April 23rd, I had my first inflation. Dr. Orringer inserted a needle into the porthole of the expander and before my very eyes I saw my breasts expand to an approximate full A cup. It is a freaky process and incredibly uncomfortable. For the first couple of days after being inflated, I felt sore and tingly. The nerve endings on the inside of my arms felt like they were on fire. It was the most uncomfortable sensation. I could not rest my arms at my side. I walked around with my hands on my stomach with my arms extended out. I couldn't stand anything touching them.

The cold also made my breasts tingle. I wasn't wearing a bra, so any kind of exposure made my skin crawl. Was I having phantom pains? I had read that amputees experienced that sensation with a loss of limb. Maybe it was the same for any loss of a body part. My chiropractor and acupuncturist told me my body had experienced a significant trauma and was healing itself. It would just take time.

Acupuncture definitely helped alleviate some of those tingly sensations. I had my first acupuncture treatment nine days after surgery. It was a godsend for me. My acupuncturist, Dr. Mao Ni, gave me anti-cancer herbs in the form of a capsule. He said I should take them for a minimum of five years. No reason why east shouldn't meet west in treating my disease.

Chiropractic sessions with Dr. Guy Armstrong rounded out my holistic approach to renewed health. Dr. Armstrong specializes in cranial sacral therapy, which erases the restrictions in the nerve passages. It left me feeling relaxed, renewed and energized, as if the toxic energy in my body had been released. Dr. Armstrong focused on releasing the aftereffects of general anesthesia, which can linger for weeks and months in some patients.

My first big challenge was driving. I got behind the wheel thirteen days after surgery, and it felt so awkward. My arms were still stiff and sore from surgery and I did not have the same range of motion, but I managed to drive the ten miles to Santa Monica to see Dr. Mao. I was back in the world, off pain meds and beginning to feel like my old self. Still fatigued by the end of the day, but for the most part pretty good.

23 DOUBLE WHAMMY

Dr. Funk had recommended two oncologists, Dr. Philomena McAndrew and a former colleague at Cedars Sinai. Dr. McAndrew is probably the most well-known breast cancer specialist in L.A., having treated a high profile clientele including, most recently, Christina Applegate. She appeared on the Oprah Winfrey show with Christina, which made her a household name. When I called her office I was informed there was a month long wait. That seemed like an eternity to me. A close friend recommended I consult with an oncology group in Santa Monica. I was able to get in to see the resident breast cancer specialist right away.

Big Al and I met with her on April 29th, fifteen days after my surgery. The offices were lovely, catering to the patient, including a chemo room that overlooks the Pacific and an art room for therapy. Not that I have ever been a doodler, but for some people that might be a therapeutic diversion.

The doctor was very straightforward and seemed optimistic about my case. Due to the one positive node, she recommended four rounds of chemo including TC (Taxotere and Cytoxin), followed by five years on an aromatase inhibitor, an anti-estrogen drug like Tamoxifen. Tamoxifen is typically given to pre-menopausal women and Arimidex or Femara is given to post-menopausal patients. I was considered post-menopausal since I did not have ovaries and had discontinued my estrogen. My body would be getting a double whammy, since I just stopped taking the estrogen prior to surgery and would now be taking an estrogen inhibitor. I would begin taking Arimidex after I completed the four rounds of chemo. She made it all sound so matter of fact. The biggest downside was hair loss. No getting around that.

When I mentioned I was waiting for the results of my MammaPrint she glossed over that, saying the test is for node-negative patients. She did not say if those results would impact my course of treatment. She also did not suggest I have an Oncotype DX test. Later, that would prove puzzling.

An Oncotype DX is a twenty-one gene assay that provides an individualized prediction of chemotherapy benefit and ten year distant recurrence in certain women with early stage breast cancer. It is done in the United States and is performed on a frozen tissue specimen. It is recommended for use in newly diagnosed estrogen receptor positive, node-negative Stage I and II breast cancer patients, and for node-positive Stage I and II patients who are post-menopausal. I was the latter. At the time of my visit with the oncologist I had never heard of the test. I'll never know why she did not order it for me. It would have saved a lot of time and alleviated a great deal of the stress and worry in the process.

The oncologist said I could begin treatment after Ally's graduation as long as it was within a six-week window of my surgery. She briefly examined me and sent me on my way knowing I would be getting a second opinion.

I could tell Big Al was struggling with this new information. Everything had changed so quickly in our lives and now our days were consumed with doctor appointments and conversations about chemo. Our evenings were occupied with discussions about breast cancer ad nauseum. I could see I was beginning to wear Big Al down. He would often bury his head in his computer and although he was sitting right next to me, he might as well have been on another planet. I wanted him to be emotionally available 24/7 whether I needed him or not, but I quickly learned it was best not to have any expectation from him or anyone else. He was doing the best he could under the circumstances.

The next day Big Al and I met with an oncologist at Cedars-Sinai. He did not examine me. Instead, he referenced a bunch of statistical data from a site on his computer. He said if I did not have any further treatment, I would have a 30% chance of recurrence to my bones, brain, liver or lungs. An aromatase inhibitor would reduce my risk by 15% and chemotherapy would reduce it another 4-5%, which meant I would have a 10% chance of recurrence.

He recommended six rounds of chemo, including FEC (5- Fluorouracil, Epirubicin and Cyclophosphamide), followed by an aromatase inhibitor for at least five years. The oncologist had a master's degree in genetics and felt strongly that women with a BRCA1 or BRCA2 gene should be treated differently. In his opinion four rounds of chemo would not be enough. When I told him I was waiting for the results of my MammaPrint, he mentioned it was only useful in node-negative women and highly doubted my result would be favorable. It bothered me that he did not take the time to examine me. On the positive side, when I sent him follow-up emails with additional questions he got back to me within thirty minutes. Accessibility is something to be valued in a doctor.

I dissolved into tears the moment we left Cedars. I thought oncology was a black and white science and there was a standard protocol for treating early stage breast cancer. Why would the two oncologists I met with offer up differing opinions regarding treatment? I immediately got on the phone with my brother Jerry and asked him to do some research. Jerry is the Head of Immunology Development for Centocor, a division of Johnson & Johnson. Through a colleague at work he was able to get a recommendation from an oncologist at the University of Pennsylvania. She agreed with the first oncologist I met with who believed four rounds of TC should do the trick. She inquired about the results of my Oncotype DX test, although with one positive node she would not change her opinion. That was the first time I heard of an Oncotype DX.

I'm not sure why I didn't research it immediately or ask the oncologist about it. Looking back, I was overwhelmed with information, and I trusted my doctor assuming she would order the right tests. I had made my decision. I would be going with the Santa Monica oncologist. Problem solved, or so I thought.

I called the doctor on Thursday to let her know I wanted her to be my oncologist. When I did not hear back from her by the next day, I called again. Still no response other than to find out she is not in the clinic on Fridays. By Monday at noon, when I still had not received a return call, I contacted the office manager to let her know I was not successful in reaching the doctor. A phone call from the oncologist soon followed.

Accessibility to one's doctor is critical. To wait five days for a return call should have been my first indication that the Santa Monica oncologist was not the right doctor for me. I would soon get other clear-cut signs I should search for another oncologist. In the meantime, I told her about the research I had done and that I felt good about my decision to select her as my doctor. I told her how important it was for me to be able to reach her. She said she had been unusually busy and had every intention of calling me that day. I decided to give her a hall pass this time. I was eager to get the process started and felt relieved I had made a decision. I would begin chemo on Thursday, May 21st, four days after we returned from Ally's graduation.

24 EPIPHANY

Wednesday, May 6th was a huge turning point for me. I had my second appointment with Dr. Orringer for another inflation. As I was sitting in his waiting room I called home to retrieve phone messages. There was a call from Dr. Funk's office. Her nurse practitioner, Courtney, called me with great news. My MammaPrint came back very favorable. It showed I had a low rate of breast cancer recurrence. What exactly did that mean? Did I not have to have chemo now? I called Courtney back from the hallway outside Dr. Orringer's office, my heart beating out of my chest. She sounded so pleased to give me the positive results. When I asked her how that would impact my course of treatment, she said I needed to review the results with my oncologist. Since the test was typically done for node-negative women it seemed reasonable the results would not apply to me since I was node-positive.

Nonetheless, I felt incredibly blessed with this unexpected news. After being inflated to a small B cup, I made my way over to the Church of the Good Shepherd, a few blocks from Orringer's office. I felt compelled to light candles in memory of my parents. And that is when I had my mind-blowing epiphany.

It had been decades since I had walked into a Catholic church. I was raised Roman Catholic and had attended Catholic school through high school. I had been a self-proclaimed recovering Catholic since my mother died, but never went anywhere without a rosary in my purse or car. When I married Big Al we agreed to raise our children as Reform Jews. I considered converting, but knew I could not change who I was at my spiritual core.

I'm not sure I will ever be able to intellectually explain what happened that day at the Church of the Good Shepherd. As I walked into the church an overwhelming spiritual presence washed over me. It was the first time I could recall being in a church all alone, but I did not feel alone. I sat down in the first pew in front of the altar and dissolved into a puddle of tears, the kind of tears that are difficult to breathe through. I prayed to God and the Blessed Mother as if they were there, and then I was certain they *were* there. I felt at peace for the first time in weeks and knew everything would be okay if I surrendered and believed. I know that's probably difficult for some people to grasp, but for me it was truly life-changing. I finally understood my mother's steadfast faith. During my ordeal I never prayed to be cured. I prayed for courage, guidance and the wisdom to make smart decisions. My prayers had been answered.

I lit two candles in memory of my mother and father and placed them in front of the Blessed Mother. Ironically, both of my parents passed away in the month of May. Every year as May approached my sad memories resurfaced and I trudged through the month with a heavy heart. I had felt forsaken by the Blessed Mother when my mom and dad died during the month dedicated to her by the Catholic Church. I now knew she had not forsaken me. It was I who had stopped believing when my grief became unbearable. Now in my most difficult time she was there to welcome me back. I would become a regular at Sunday morning mass and it would be my favorite time of the week for meditation, reflection and prayer. I felt incredibly blessed, spiritually renewed and grateful to be back where I belonged.

When I got home that Wednesday afternoon, I called my oncologist to ask her to interpret my MammaPrint results. I wanted to know how they would impact my treatment options. By Thursday midday I still had not heard back from her. I placed another call to her, as did Big Al, but still no response. It was so frustrating, to say the least.

I had lunch with my dear friend Karen that day and shared my roller coaster ride with her. Karen probably understands me better than anyone else. She lost her mother at an early age to ovarian cancer. She also had a prophylactic hysterectomy without knowing whether or not she had the gene. We had commiserated for years about our lousy genetic history and clung to each other for encouragement and strength. It wasn't easy raising our children without the support of a mother. We understood each other well and would become like sisters over the years.

Karen is not one to let grass grow under her feet. She easily makes a preemptive strike whenever it's indicated. In her opinion, having the

MammaPrint results seemed to be muddying the water, considering they weren't validated in node-positive women. Karen thought I should be as aggressive as possible and still have the chemo regardless of the test results. She said she didn't want me to look back and regret another decision, and neither did I. But the fact is, not all women benefit equally from chemotherapy and in my opinion, the benefits had to outweigh the risks. I knew Karen would be there to support me regardless of my decision.

I dashed right from lunch to the hairdresser. I had scheduled an appointment to cut my long locks. I was beginning to prep for chemo, knowing I would eventually buzz my hair. In order to acclimate, I would do it in stages and this was the first one. In retrospect, I should have waited, but I really did not think the MammaPrint results would change my course of treatment. Besides, cutting my hair was a metaphor for cutting out the cancer. It felt good.

By late Thursday when I still hadn't heard back from my oncologist I started getting annoyed. I knew she would not be in the clinic on Friday so I was eager to reach her. By mid-Friday I felt I had no choice but to reach out to the office manager to again gain her assistance in reaching the doctor.

Within minutes the doctor called me from her car. She apologized for not phoning earlier, admitting she had been very busy. She sounded completely overwhelmed and mentioned she was on her way out of town to visit an ailing relative. She obviously had a lot on her plate, but that did not excuse her for failing to get back to patients in a timely manner.

When I asked her to interpret my MammaPrint results she said they were very favorable, however, since they had only been validated in node-negative women she recommended ordering an Oncotype DX. If that test concurred with the MammaPrint, then having chemo would be like taking a sledgehammer to an ant. Great news! I may not have to have chemo after all. I'm not sure why the doctor waited until the MammaPrint results came back to order the Oncotype DX. When I mentioned the lack of accessibility to her was troublesome for me she got defensive. Not cool in my book. It was apparent to me we were not a match made in heaven. I felt compelled to seek consults with other oncologists.

25 AVRUM BLUMING

I called Dr. Orringer and asked for his advice regarding an oncologist. He highly recommended Avrum Bluming, a general oncologist whose practice was made up of 60% breast cancer patients. He was located in Encino, near my home. He also recommended James Waisman, a well-known and respected breast cancer specialist with offices in Hawthorne, California. Waisman was geographically undesirable, however, in retrospect that should never have entered into my decision.

Once again Big Al stepped in to help out. Dr. Bluming is affiliated with Tarzana Regional Medical Center and Big Al has a close friend who is a radiologist there. He put a call into Dr. Bluming and within minutes I had an appointment for the following Monday morning, May 11th. Dr. Bluming did not know us from Adam, but he still called Big Al back within ten minutes. That's what I mean about accessibility.

That weekend I was on edge. I was happy I had been thrown this curve ball, but what would it all mean? I was eager to get the Oncotype test done. It's a very expensive test; approximately $3,800, and a patient has to meet specific criteria in order to gain approval. My oncologist said she would immediately order it, but I found out the following week it had slipped through the cracks. Aggravating to say the least.

In the meantime, I would meet with Avrum Bluming, a gifted physician and extraordinary human being who would change my life in unexpected ways. Big Al and I went to his office Monday morning. We filled out the requisite forms, were ushered to his private office and waited for him to arrive.

Avrum Bluming looks as unique as his name. He has an intense presence with piercing eyes, and has undoubtedly lived his life to the fullest, as evidenced by the many photographs and artifacts in his office.

He conducted the most thorough medical history of all of the doctors I had met with. He covered everything and asked very pointed questions about my past. Some of them were uncomfortable. I felt as though I was being interrogated, but quickly realized this man was a hunter and gatherer of comprehensive data and I appreciated his thoroughness. When he was done with his extensive questioning, he asked me to move to an examination room. Under my breath I grumbled to Big Al that I was tired of being examined. Why couldn't he just give us his opinion based on my records and the information I gave him? Big Al told me to quit being a baby and just do it. Dr. Bluming looked me over from top to bottom. When finished, he asked me to get dressed and meet him in his office.

I was convinced Dr. Bluming would recommend chemo. I was wrong. He explained that at best chemo would increase my disease-free survival by 1.7%.

And then he stood up, leaned on his desk and said with conviction, "I do not recommend chemo in your case."

My head was spinning. What did he just say? No chemo? How could he make that recommendation without the Oncotype DX result? He said he did not need the Oncotype test or the MammaPrint. He based his decision on my Mitotic Index (MI) score, which was a one out of three. The MI is a measurement of the rate at which cells divide; the higher the MI, the more aggressive the cancer. It is determined by how many mitotic figures the pathologist can see in the microscope field. Dr. Bluming also referenced my KI-67 Antigen score of 19%, considered an intermediate score. It is used to evaluate proliferative activity. A breast tumor that scores high is made of cells that are rapidly growing. The KI score is also a prognostic marker in early stage breast cancer. He said if mine had been 80% he would feel differently. Then I asked him if he was just telling me what I wanted to hear.

He responded emphatically, "That would be criminal, for me to do that to a patient."

In my case the benefits of chemo did not outweigh the risks and he believed it would have little to no impact on my disease. I asked him if his recommendation would be any different if I were his wife or daughter. His daughter's wedding picture was proudly displayed in his office. He took my breath away when he said, both his wife and daughter had breast cancer and he would tell them the same thing. Tears welled up in my eyes. This man had walked the talk and his personal experience and compassion filled his office. I trusted everything he said with my whole being.

The only downside to Dr. Bluming was that he was not a provider with my health insurance company. When I told him that would present a financial obstacle for us, he leaned back in his chair and said, "I have made enough money in my lifetime. I have milk in the fridge and bread on my table. I would gladly accept whatever your insurance will pay." I wanted to kiss his feet. Unfortunately, the tests he would order on an ongoing basis would be out of network and enormously expensive. That was out of the question, considering Dr. Waisman was an approved provider. I had no choice but to meet Dr. Waisman.

I will never forget Avrum Bluming's sage advice. He could see I was troubled by some of the foolhardy decisions I had made. He told me to stop looking back and beating myself up.

At one point he said, "So you think the estrogen you took all those years caused your cancer? Well, it didn't."

I had to let go. No amount of self-flagellation would erase the past. It was most important to make smart decisions now.

I wrote Avrum Bluming a note and gave him a copy of <u>One God Clapping: The Spiritual Path of a Zen Rabbi</u> by Alan Lew. I sensed he was a spiritual man and I felt strongly he would appreciate the book. There is a passage that clearly defines how I felt about him:

"No one in our lives is superfluous: everyone who appears has something indispensable to teach us, without which our life could not go forward."

Avrum Bluming left a profound imprint on my life. I entered his office feeling overwhelmed and confused and left empowered and hopeful. He is a man of immeasurable kindness and compassion. If I did not know better I would swear he is an angel disguised in a white coat, parceling out pearls of wisdom and guidance to those in need. I will be forever grateful for having the opportunity to meet him.

26 ANGELS ABOUND

I called Dr. Waisman's office the minute I got home from seeing Dr. Bluming. I spoke to Cami, his assistant, and for the first time found out how a front office should work. She was incredible. Cami is a take-charge woman who knows exactly how to manage a patient struggling with the anxieties of a very cumbersome process. I told Cami where I had been and what doctors I had consulted with. I let her know my oncologist had ordered an Oncotype DX. She said Dr. Waisman would see me after I had the results. I expected to have them by the end of the week so I was hoping to schedule my appointment for the week of May 18th, after we returned from Ally's graduation. Cami could not have been more accommodating.

After we spoke she took it upon herself to call my oncologist's office to make sure they forwarded the Oncotype results. That's when she discovered the frozen tissue specimen still hadn't been sent from Cedars-Sinai to Genomic Health, the company that administers the Oncotype DX. Cami called me immediately to inform me of the situation. I was perplexed to say the least. My oncologist told me the Friday before that she would order it immediately. I had no clue what the hold up was.

Apparently my oncologist's assistant had not put the correct paperwork in place to requisition the frozen specimen and get approval from my insurance company. Big Al and I were exasperated. At that point we would have paid for the test ourselves, but it's not that simple. A physician still must order the test. Big Al got on the phone with the insurance company and spoke to the head nurse. He did all he could to put a rush on the approval process, but everything lay in the hands of my oncologist's office. Just when we were about to pull our hair out, another angel appeared.

A new neighbor was moving into the house two doors down from us. She happened to be standing in the middle of our cul-de-sac as we were leaving to go out to dinner that night. I introduced myself to be polite, not expecting a lengthy conversation. She blurted out she was completely overwhelmed renovating her new house. She had three children, including newborn twins, and worked full time for Genomic Health, the company that administers the Oncotype DX test. Now what are the odds of something like that happening? Angels seemed to be all around me.

When I told her about my predicament with the Oncotype DX she volunteered her assistance in expediting the process. So now I had Cami and my new neighbor acting as my advocates. My neighbor later informed me my insurance company initially denied the precertification. That made no sense. Although the test was expensive, it would be a whole lot cheaper for the insurance company to pay for that versus the enormous expense of chemotherapy treatments. The test might negate the need for chemotherapy. My oncologist had to do what's called a peer-to-peer assessment and speak directly to the Medical Director at my insurance company explaining why I was a candidate for the test. Luck was on my side, and the test was finally approved.

Unfortunately all of the back and forth wrangling delayed things another week, which meant postponing my visit with Waisman. It was now Wednesday, May 15th, four long weeks since my surgery. For now everything was on hold. On Thursday, Big Al and I would leave for Pennsylvania. Graduation day was here and mama bear was on her way.

27 GRADUATION

I cannot begin to describe the gratitude and joy I felt as I traveled to my daughter's graduation. I was grateful to God to be making this journey, when just a few short weeks before I wasn't certain if I would have the strength to make the trip. I was experiencing so many emotions, not to mention the unexpected feelings I encountered while flying.

I have always been a white-knuckle flyer, typically drugging myself with Xanax to alleviate my fear of running up and down the aisles shrieking with my hair on end. It's always been more of a claustrophobic and lack of control issue versus fear of crashing and dying. Since my diagnosis I realized how foolish phobias are. Nothing is in our control anyway. So I boarded the plane as a fatalist for the first time in my life. The Xanax was buried deep within my carryon and I had no intention of needing it.

What I did not expect was the uncomfortable feeling in my chest that seemed to worsen the longer I was in flight. My new set of twins felt like a couple of bags of expanding potato chips, hot and tingly all over. I kept pulling my shirt away from my chest. Big Al thought I was crazy and told me to relax. Easy for him to say. I wonder how he would feel if his balls suddenly expanded mid-air? The feeling seemed to dissipate once we landed in Baltimore. So I forgot about it.

We were eager to pick up our car rental for the one and a half hour drive to Lancaster. I could not wait to see Ally and Matt. There's no doubt I was beginning to tire, but I would get a second wind. We met the kids at college row, where Ally shared an apartment with three girls. They were so happy and relieved to see me. Their mama bear looked the same except for shorter hair. We went downstairs to a local brewery for dinner and had some much needed family time. It would be a whirlwind of a weekend so we would make the first night an early one.

Graduations are bittersweet. Ready to move on, yet difficult to say goodbye to friends you have shared the past four years with. I could see the conflict in Ally's eyes. I know she was eager to return to Los Angeles and get on with the next phase in her life, but she would be 3,000 miles away from many of the close friends she had made during her years at Franklin & Marshall. I knew, however, she was glad to be coming home for me.

After dinner, Matt went to say goodbye to some freshmen friends and Ally came back to the hotel with us. I was exhausted by then and ready to get out of my clothes. I had a favorite nightshirt that Marylou gave me when I got out of the hospital. It's an oversized button down men's shirt that proved to be the most comfortable item of clothing after my surgery. I highly recommend one for any woman having a mastectomy. I wore it every night and most days when I was around the house. As I removed my top I caught a glimpse of myself in the mirror. I was shocked to see my breasts were completely red. Maybe that was the end result of all that discomfort on the plane. I thought about calling my plastic surgeon, but shrugged it off, knowing I would address it with him when I got back. I would later find out it was just a little swelling that had occurred due to the altitude while in flight. The discoloration would dissipate over time. For now, it was all about Ally.

After I crawled into bed, Ally stayed for a while, making sure I was okay before going to a party with fellow graduates. It was so indescribably great to be back in Pennsylvania with my children. I was able to put the thought of test results and pending treatment out of my mind for the first time in weeks. Sometimes you need to get away to get out of your own head.

I woke up Friday feeling refreshed and ready to tackle the day. We ventured into downtown Lancaster for lunch and some family time. Ally was looking forward to Saturday's events, including graduation and a luncheon with our extended family. My brother Jerry and his wife Diane would be in attendance, along with Big Al's brother Howard and his family. We were thrilled they were flying in from L.A. for the festivities. I knew it was going to be one of those surreal experiences in life. To think: thirty-one years before I had graduated from the same college and my brother was a member of the Class of '73, thirty-six years ago. We would be three for three from Franklin & Marshall College. In another three years, Matt would hopefully round out the group. We were very proud of our legacy at F & M.

We had a lovely family dinner the evening before graduation at Rosa Rosa, our favorite Italian restaurant in Lancaster. We ate like kings, shared some vino and relished in Ally's wonderful accomplishment. In that moment, I did not have a care in the world. I was solely focused on the celebration at hand. I knew once I saw my brother the next day, we would share conversation about my pending treatment. For now, we talked about our days at F & M and how in thirty-one years the more things changed, the more they had stayed the same.

The morning of graduation I changed ten times. I wanted to wear something comfortable and presentable. It was hot and humid outside, with the weather calling for showers at any moment. I was wearing a black pantsuit, but could not seem to find the right top. Big Al thought I should wear a button-down white blouse, but the fabric was annoying me. I tried on a sleeveless black and white top with a plunging neckline and I could tell by the look on Big Al's face that he did not approve. He said it made me look flat-chested. Well, I *was* flat-chested and really didn't give a damn. The black and white shirt was much more comfortable and that's the one I chose to wear.

We made our way to the graduation site and searched for Howard and family in the crowd. Fortunately they had arrived earlier and secured decent seats midway through the audience. Just as we sat down we saw my brother and Diane in the distance, looking for us amidst the throngs of people. It felt good to see Jer and I know he was reassured to see me looking as well as I did. Colin Powell was the graduation speaker and we were all excited to hear his speech. The stage was set up in the exact spot it was the year I graduated. I was experiencing flashbacks galore.

As the graduates marched in we craned our necks to spot Ally amongst her classmates. Big Al and I could not believe our little Ally "cat" was graduating from college; a dream come true. One of my greatest fears had been erased. I made it to my daughter's graduation.

Excited as I was to be there, I glanced over and saw my brother and Matt, sound asleep with their heads drooping over. Unbelievable! Graduations, however, can be long and boring. Just as they were about to call Ally's name, a light wind blew through the trees. My sister-in-law Diane looked over at me and said, "Do you think your mom and dad are here today?" I had no doubt they were smiling down on all of us. I could feel their presence all around. And in that moment Ally Bianchina, named after her father and grandmother, crossed the stage, moved her tassel to the right side and collected her diploma from General Colin

Powell. I glanced over at Big Al and he was grinning from ear to ear. We were immensely proud of our baby girl.

After the requisite picture taking and long goodbyes with Ally's professors and friends, we made our way over to the Stockyard Inn. The lengthy graduation ceremony left us all in need of sustenance and libation. I sat next to my brother so we could finally have a chance to talk. I told him about the MammaPrint and the Oncotype DX and the fact that the test results might change my treatment options. He seemed skeptical considering I had the one positive node, but agreed we would discuss it once the final results were back. I got the feeling he thought I was trying to weasel my way out of chemo. Aside from our brief conversation the rest of the luncheon was all about celebrating Ally, the new graduate and fellow F & M alum.

We flew home the next day, happy to have our baby bears with us. I was ecstatic Ally would be back in L.A. for good. No more tearful goodbyes at the airport and long months without seeing each other. She had grown into an independent, mature and beautiful young woman during her four years away. She was glad to be returning to L.A. and certain this was where she wanted to begin her career. Selfishly, I was relieved she would be home again. Ally and I have always been two peas in a pod. I knew she would be the best medicine in the world for me.

The following week dragged on as I waited for the Oncotype DX results. My neighbor was doing everything she could to expedite the test. For now, my chemotherapy, which was supposed to begin on May 21st, was postponed. I had an appointment scheduled with Dr. Waisman for Wednesday, May 27th, six weeks after my surgery. I felt like we were under the gun and one way or the other had to make a decision about chemo as soon as possible.

I tried to stay busy and enjoy Memorial Day weekend, but my thoughts were never far from the Oncotype test. I hoped it would concur with the MammaPrint. On Tuesday, May 26th, I called Cami at Dr. Waisman's office to find out if they had the results. She said they received them on Friday, but could not give them to me over the phone. Dr. Waisman would review them with me in person the following day. That's when I discovered my oncologist had my results and did not have the decency to call me. It would have saved me all the stress and worry over the holiday weekend.

I understand oncologists have difficult jobs and I can only imagine the pressure they must be under; however, there is no excuse for not getting back to a patient with important test results as soon as possible. Every day seems like an eternity when you are waiting for information regarding your health, especially when you have recently been diagnosed with cancer. Although frustrating, it was no surprise I could not reach my oncologist prior to meeting with Dr. Waisman. At least I only had to get through one more night until I had my answers.

The drive down to Dr. Waisman's offices in Hawthorne took about a half hour, not as bad as I anticipated. It seemed ridiculous I had not consulted with him earlier because I thought he was geographically undesirable. I felt being close to home was important when undergoing chemo. That should not have been part of my equation. It's the relationship with the physician that matters most.

The minute I walked into Dr. Waisman's office I knew I was in the right place. The name of his practice is Breastlink and it is 100% devoted to patients with breast cancer. Their single goal is to deliver optimal care to women, including treatment of the *whole* woman. They have an excellent team of oncologists in addition to psychotherapists, researchers and patient advocates. On the lighter side, it's easy to find parking, which by the way is free, and their offices are located on the second floor, which can be accessed by stairs. No walking into an overwhelming impersonal hospital facility, navigating your way around a maze of parking lots, only to find yourself in an elevator with too many people in a cancer center with all kinds of patients. Psychologically I found it much better to be in a facility dedicated to breast cancer patients.

Lori, at the front desk, greeted my husband and me as if we were her long lost friends. It was similar to the experience I had at Dr. Funk's and Dr. Orringer's offices. We eagerly waited to meet Dr. Waisman and we were not disappointed. He has such a kind, compassionate way about him. We clicked immediately. He examined me first and then asked us to meet him in his private office.

My heart was pounding out of my chest until Dr. Waisman said the words I was hoping for.

"Your Oncotype DX score was fifteen, which means your cancer has a low rate of recurrence and chemotherapy would have minimal to no impact on your disease."

I asked him how accurate the test was in node-positive women and in how many patients it had been validated. He said the results were from a clinical study involving 367 patients. The study included post-menopausal female patients with node-positive, hormone receptor positive breast cancer. That did not sound like a lot of patients to me, and was not reassuring.

Dr. Waisman noted that prior to 2005, any woman with a tumor greater than one centimeter automatically had chemo, but since that time with the advent of MammaPrint and Oncotype DX, they had found all women did not benefit equally from chemo. He believed I would get the greatest benefit from Femara, an aromatase inhibitor that would suppress any estrogen production. How could I be producing estrogen if I did not have ovaries and had discontinued my HRT? Unbeknownst to me, the adrenal glands also produce estrogen. Femara would block that production. Although I would not be having chemo, it was not as if I would be getting off scot-free from taking any harsh medications. Femara is a powerful drug with its own potential risks and side effects and I would be taking it for at least five years.

I was finally hearing exactly what I wanted, but still felt concerned. Funny thing about cancer: it robs you of your peace of mind. Dr. Waisman said he would still administer the chemotherapy if I wanted it, but he would not feel good about giving it to me. The risks of the chemo would outweigh the benefits in my case. Big Al and I were ecstatic, though not quite ready to celebrate. Dr. Waisman asked my permission to call my oncologist to see if she concurred. He was able to reach her and confirmed she was on the same page.

When we left his office, I had a message from my former oncologist on my cell phone. She said she had great news. I did not need chemo after all. I saved her message and listened to it countless times. What a relief! Six weeks and one day after my double mastectomy, I finally had a plan.

After sending out a brief text that read "No Chemo" to several close friends, I called my brother to share the news. I also wanted to get his opinion on my situation.

He said, "You have to make a decision you can live with down the road regardless of the outcome. If your cancer recurs someday, you cannot look back with regret that you did not have the chemo. My only other concern is our family is so unlucky, and for that reason alone you may want to do it. It's just four rounds and I think you would do well."

I knew exactly what he was saying. I was already kicking myself for not having the prophylactic mastectomies. He himself had advised against it. Now I was getting another opportunity to make the "right" decision, and he did not want me to blow it.

The fact is, no one has a crystal ball in life. I had sought the expertise of three well-respected oncologists and they all concurred. It would have saved me a lot of time and aggravation if the Oncotype DX test had been ordered from day one, because then chemo would never have been on the table. I was benefiting from cutting edge technology and had to make my decision based on the information at hand. I could not make it based on dated studies that did not apply to me. I would trust Dr. Waisman, take a leap of faith and begin taking my new magic pill, Femara, the next day.

29 SIDE EFFECTS

In typical OCD fashion, I continued to lose sleep over my decision. Why couldn't things be black and white? I was allowing that one positive node to drive me insane. My own mind would continue to be the bane of my existence if I allowed it. In other words, I had to let go of the things I could not control or I would end up being my own worst enemy.

And then, just as I was beginning to feel big and strong again, the lovely side effects from Femara kicked in, including hot flashes, fatigue, insomnia, joint pain, mood swings, and my personal favorite, a non-existent libido. One minute I would be laughing and freezing and the next bursting into tears and disrobing. My family thought I was losing my mind. My even going personality was replaced with a bad case of PMS on steroids. Ambien and Melatonin would address the sleeplessness, but the rest of the side effects would rage on for months.

Needless to say, I was grateful to be alive and had a greater appreciation for each day. I hadn't planned on feeling like I was eighty years old, however. That's the dirty little secret of aromatase inhibitors that doctors will gloss over: they sneak up on you and try to steal the quality of your life. If Femara kept my cancer from recurring however, then the side effects would be well worth it.

Exercise proved to be the antidote by stimulating my lagging energy level as well as loosening up my stiff joints and tight muscles. I also slept much better on the days I worked out. I began riding the recumbent bike on level one for thirty minutes a day. I took baby steps, which was frustrating for me, since I'm typically in whirling dervish mode. I also worked out with a trainer who took me through a series of slow stretching exercises and lightweight resistance repetitions.

Michael Pauldine did more than stretch my limbs. He motivated me and gave me a safe place to vent about my aches, pains and frustrations, allowing me to maintain my dignity as I grimaced and cried through the pain. He could see I was self-conscious about the way I looked and felt. He encouraged me to take time to heal and not push my body beyond its limitations.

My right side, where my lymph nodes had been removed, was extremely tight. I was still struggling with my range of motion and by the end of the day could barely lift my shirt over my head. Squeezing a lemon on top of my old fashioned manual juicer was nearly impossible. I had to stand on my tiptoes and use the full weight of my body. There was a simple solution for that. My friend Karen told me to get with the program and go buy one of those handheld juicers that require little effort to squeeze. There was no need to get frustrated with such a small task.

I had to work a lot harder on the overhead movements. I only had ten sessions with Michael, but they were enough to get me back on track. It took several months before I could lift a sweater or shirt over my head with ease. When it finally happened it almost went unnoticed, until Big Al remarked that I didn't need his help anymore. Mission accomplished.

In the meantime, I would see Dr. Orringer two more times, on June 1st and June 25th, to continue inflating my expanders to the desired size of the implants I wanted. Each visit resulted in a couple of days of discomfort, but by then I was used to the drill. I was bordering on a large B, small C cup and was looking very Dolly Partonesque for me. I was afraid if a strong wind came along I might find myself sailing across the western sky. I knew I was big when friends would see me and exclaim, "Whoa, you look completely different!" My breasts were practically in my throat and stuck out far enough to set a martini glass on them. I was uncomfortable and had lost my symmetry. I knew I had to downsize with my permanent implants. I scheduled my surgery for July 24th, three months after my mastectomies.

I met with Dr. Waisman for a six-week checkup on July 6th. Driving down to his office stirred up a lot of stuff, but I managed to keep it together. He examined me and did a CA15-3 (Cancer Antigen 15-3) blood test, which is a tumor marker used to monitor certain cancers, especially breast cancer. An elevated CA 15-3 is sometimes associated with an increased chance of early recurrence in breast cancer. Dr. Waisman's nurse practitioner told me that typically, the test would not show an elevation so soon after diagnosis. I found that reassuring.

When I told Dr. Waisman I had morphed into Jekyll and Hyde, he said the symptoms from Femara would probably level out somewhere around five months. That seemed like an eternity to me and I wasn't sure my family could put up with my new attitude for that long, but they proved to be incredibly patient with me. Half the time I think they just ignored my mood swings, chalking it up to the new magic pill. I must say I was quite dramatic for a few months, getting hysterical for the most ridiculous reasons. And God forbid I should hear a story about breast cancer, or read something online or in a magazine. That would set me off for days. My visit with Dr. Waisman went well and I would learn shortly thereafter that my blood test was within the normal range. I would see him again in three months.

When I met with Dr. Orringer on July 7th, I was shocked to find him in a sling. He had taken a fall in his home and tore the rotator cuff on his right side. He assured me he was fine and would have assistance in the operating room if need be. I, of course took that as a divine sign to postpone. At that point I was in desperate need of a timeout from the hair-raising roller coaster ride I had been on the past three months.

I called Big Al when I left Orringer's office and told him I wanted to delay the implant procedure for at least another month. What was the rush? I had finished my inflations, ending with 500 cc of saline in the expanders. I wanted the opportunity to be certain they were the right size for me. I was also in desperate need to get out of Dodge.

31 ALOHA

Big Al suggested a trip to Maui, my favorite place to unwind and relax. I could postpone my surgery until the end of summer, and join my family for a much needed vacation. Orringer agreed it would be no problem to reschedule. Ana Marie, his office manager, said it was perfect timing to go away and rejuvenate.

So I postponed my surgery until August 20th, and took off for Maui for nine days at the end of July. I was reluctant to put a bathing suit on, for about five minutes. Being anonymous gives you the courage to do almost anything. The truth is I hadn't looked that good in a bathing suit in years. I had lost ten lbs. since I was diagnosed, and I had a new set of very perky boobs. For the first time in months, I felt confident and good about myself. I walked every morning, swam in the ocean each day and completely let go while there. For a minute I forgot about breast cancer and the rocky road I had just traveled. Time away with my family in a place we all loved was exactly what I needed. The pictures from that trip belie what I had just been through. They look no different from past vacations in Maui. We women are a resilient bunch.

We returned home in time to celebrate my 53rd birthday. My family took me to Pace, a charming restaurant in Laurel Canyon, for dinner. I reminded them a year before we had dined at Il Grano on my birthday.

On that day, as the waiter brought my birthday cake for the ceremonial song, the candle blew out before he placed it in front of me. I knew immediately it was a bad sign. It completely freaked me out. My family said I was being my typical, unfounded superstitious self. But they did not have my keen intuition. When I shared what happened with my friend Caryn she said maybe it was my mother blowing out the candle as a sign that she was there. A nice thought, but I didn't buy it. Unfortunately I was right, because my 52nd year turned out to be a wild ride from hell, but with a lot of heaven mixed in too.

So this time my family made sure the waiter put the cake down in front me and *then* lit the candle. They were nervous wrecks until I blew it out with gusto, making a very important wish. My 53rd year began with all good vibes.

By early August, I was feeling much stronger on the heels of an incredible vacation. I had a brief respite where the only appointments I had were with my acupuncturist and chiropractor. They did a world of good nursing me back to health. It felt amazing to have a break from the routine of the preceding three months.

I rescheduled my implant surgery for August 20th, and looked forward to finally getting it done. It would be an outpatient procedure and a much easier recovery than the mastectomies. I had considered waiting one more week, until Matt went back to school, but he was hardly ever around and I had Ally to help pack him up and get him ready for his sophomore year.

Ally had been an incredible source of support to me throughout the summer months. She was in the process of looking for a job and as a fate would have it, she wouldn't land something until the end of September, which added up to a lot of time with mama bear. I know Ally suffered from anxiety during her long job search, but it gave us the opportunity to catch up on reruns of Law and Order. We were über couch potatoes and loved every minute of it. I hope she knows how grateful I am she was able to help me through the most difficult time in my life. It reminded me of time I shared with my mother. Memories like that are truly priceless.

My boychick Matt, on the other hand, was all business as usual. I appreciated the fact that he treated me like nothing had happened. It made me feel as though everything were normal. Once in a while he would pause and ask if I was doing okay. I always reassured him that his mama bear was just fine. I guess I'll always protect my baby bear.

I had my last office visit with Dr. Orringer prior to my implant surgery on August 17th. We discussed the size of the implants I wanted, in addition to saline versus silicone. I had lost sleep over that decision as well. I was leaning toward saline, my logic being that if the implants ruptured it would only be salt water that leaked into my body. The saline implants, however, are in a silicone sack, so there was no way to get around that completely. My brother Jerry helped me make my decision. He reminded me silicone implants are FDA approved, more comfortable and built to last. He wanted me to avoid unnecessary revision surgery in case the saline implants ruptured. I surprised myself at my decision to choose silicone, but in retrospect I'm happy I did.

Saline implants would have been more round in shape, less natural looking and more likely to wrinkle over time. Silicone feels more natural to the touch and softer overall. I was pleased with my decision. Next, I had to decide on the size of the implants I wanted. Dr. Orringer recommended I go with the size I currently had, which was 500 cc, a small C cup or going even larger, to 550 cc, a full C cup, but I already knew I wanted to go smaller. I wanted something that was as close to what I had before. I missed my old self.

I insisted I wanted 450 cc, which would be equivalent to a full B. Of course, in my typical analysis paralysis fashion I asked a few people close to me for their opinion, including my gynecologist. He said if I wanted to get noticed at a cocktail party I should go with a size C. That's all I needed to hear since that's not the kind of attention I would ever crave. In the end I got exactly what I wanted.

I had my implant surgery at St. John's Hospital. I was disappointed because I had hoped to go to a surgery center for the procedure, but my insurance company would not approve it. I was trying to avoid a hospital setting. St. John's is Dr. Orringer's home turf, so it worked out well. The nursing staff and anesthesiologist were great.

I expected my surgery to be three hours, but it ended up being four and a half. Dr. Orringer said he tried the larger implant, even sat me up on the operating table to take a look, but knew I would be happier with the smaller implant to complement my petite frame. Much to my chagrin I woke up to a different type of incision than expected. I thought he was just going to reopen the vertical scars created by the mastectomies; however, he made the decision while I was under to give me a lift and cut me under my breasts as well. I had incisions that looked like anchors, typically done during breast lift augmentation. We had not discussed that beforehand so I was disappointed at first, but Dr. Orringer assured me the scars would fade and the overall look of my breasts would be far superior. He removed excess skin from under my breasts from years of sagging and it really did give me a much rounder looking set of twins.

I woke up feeling some pressure and burning in my chest area. This time I *did* feel like a baby elephant was sitting on top of me. The implants are placed under the pectoral muscles, so some soreness is to be expected. For the first time in months I found myself wearing a bra. It was a zip up sports bra designed for women undergoing breast surgery. In a weird way, it felt good to be wearing my least favorite undergarment. I felt normal again. The implants were much softer than the expanders and although I could only see the top portion of my breasts peeking out, they looked so real.

I stayed in recovery for a couple of hours, fighting through some nausea from the general anesthesia. I had not experienced that after my mastectomies. I got sick to my stomach a couple times and then felt well enough to take the twins home. I thought we should have a christening and name them. Weeks later, while having lunch with my favorite priest, he suggested Itsy and Bitsy and said a prayer for my continued good health. A sense of humor never hurts.

I was anxious to unzip my bra and take a look, but decided to wait a couple of days until the drains were removed. Dr. Orringer stopped by the house to check up on me and took out the drains, and then we had the big reveal. I was blown away by how real my new breasts looked and felt. Of course, they were swollen and very numb, however I had zero bruising, which pleasantly surprised me. I know they looked different without nipples and areolas, but to me they were perfect. It's funny how you can get used to a new reality. When I looked in the mirror I saw a woman who had been reconstructed, who carried the battle scars of someone brave enough to stare down cancer and survive. Two procedures to go and I would be whole again.

While I recovered, Ally helped Matt pack up to go back to school. I'm sure Ally did all the packing and Matt barely paid attention. I was feeling apprehensive about him leaving again, but knew he was looking forward to his second year at Franklin & Marshall. I would be visiting him in mid-October with Ally for our first alumni weekend together. At least I wouldn't have to wait long before seeing him again.

Six days after surgery, I felt well enough to drive Matt to the airport. The recovery was much easier than expected. For the first time, I dropped him off curbside at LAX, missing out on our walk to the security checkpoint with a long, drawn out goodbye. Life was changing and my boychick was becoming a man. I got out of the car to give him a hug and before I knew it he was out of sight. I boo hooed all the way home. Some things in life will never change.

In the meantime, I continued to heal. Dr. Orringer removed my stitches a few weeks after my implant surgery. My reconstructed breasts looked incredibly natural minus the scars, which over time would begin to fade. I used a variety of products to diminish the scarring, but had the most success with bioCorneum, a cream Dr. Funk recommended. Although I was healing well I still had to wait at least a few months before undergoing nipple reconstruction. I had hoped to have the cherry on top sooner than that, but did not want to rush things. The nipple reconstruction and areola tattoos were minor procedures I could do anytime. The worst was behind me. I had considered foregoing the final two procedures, but have never been one to leave a job undone. By late April 2010, a little over a year after my bilateral mastectomy, I would be physically whole again. The reconstruction of my emotional self would continue to be a work in progress.

33 YOU WALK, I LIVE

In mid-September, Marylou participated in the two-day Avon Breast Cancer Walk event, walking forty miles in honor of her dear friend Penny and me. It seemed incredulous her two best friends were diagnosed around the same time. As fate would have it, I heard of several other acquaintances who were diagnosed shortly after me. It seemed as though women were coming out of the woodwork and suddenly I became the expert on breast cancer. It was almost too soon for me to be offering guidance and advice to other women. I was still in the thick of it myself. I tried to be as available as I could, but suffered setbacks mentally and emotionally whenever I heard of someone else. There was a part of me that wanted to distance myself from anything having to do with breast cancer. When Big Al got all fired up to do a climb on Mt. Shasta for breast cancer I asked him to postpone a year and give me a chance to breathe and get through all of my procedures.

Marylou, however, was on a mission. She had spent the summer training hard, walking long distances every Saturday and Sunday to get in shape. She works full time, so it wasn't easy raising the money and logging miles. I was deeply touched she put her money where her mouth was and did something to stamp out the disease that had stricken two of her close friends. She far surpassed the $1,800 entry fee and I will be forever grateful for her efforts on my behalf.

I drove down to Long Beach the second day to cheer her on along the route. It was another surreal moment, being a spectator at an event I had participated in eight years before with my amigos from Kansas. This time I was a survivor and men, women and children were walking for me. I stood alone on a side street waiting for Marylou. As each walker passed by I bowed and thanked them for their efforts and cheered them on to finish strong. They were my heroes and because they walked, I live. I was so grateful and finally understood the magnitude of giving back. I had been the giver and now I was the receiver and was incredibly moved by the generosity of spirit I witnessed that day. I saw a woman without hair who carried a sign that said, "Yesterday was my last day of chemo." I saw families walking in memory of someone they had lost. I saw small children walking with their father in honor of their mother who was a survivor. It brought back a rush of memories for me.

34 DEPRESSION

I'm not sure if my sudden onset of depression was caused by the Femara, Matt's departure, the Avon Walk or the aftereffects of surgery. It was probably a combination of everything. When I was first diagnosed I had too much to do and had no time to be depressed, except for the momentary unraveling and waterworks. I was also the center of everyone's attention in the beginning. As time went by, family and friends got back to their lives and my cancer became a minor footnote. I felt myself withdrawing and disconnecting from close friends. I had no patience for small talk about their lives and found comfort in solitude. I was still getting used to the fact I had just overcome a major health crisis. While Big Al only wanted to talk about how many days he would ski come winter, I wanted to hibernate for the season.

My three-month checkup with Dr. Waisman at the end of September was perfectly timed. When I admitted feeling withdrawn and depressed, he suggested I speak to his in-house psychotherapist, Lisa Donley. The sessions with her would be free. It is all part of their team approach to treating patients. I told Dr. Waisman I would consider calling her.

When I shared with him that I had the libido of a flea, he recommended a testosterone patch to increase my sex drive. No way I was using it, no matter how many doctors told me it was safe. My sex drive wasn't the only problem. I was dry as the Sahara Desert and my skin had become so thin, tearing easily while getting frisky. He suggested a lubricant, which to me is one big mess fest. I must admit I did go out and buy my new favorite product, Astroglide, but I longed for the good old days when Niagara Falls was more like it.

I felt like I got gypped twice in my life, having a hysterectomy so young and then the bilateral mastectomy. It definitely affected my psyche having so many female parts removed. But I knew in my heart that my sexuality came from within and in time Big Al and I would figure it out and find pleasure in unexpected ways.

The rest of my visit with him went well. His nurse practitioner took my vitals while Dr. Waisman examined my breasts, remarking that Dr. Orringer did a great job. I did not have a blood test during that visit, which was a relief, knowing I did not have to wait for a test result to come back. Dr. Waisman would see me again in six months. I was surprised he did not want to continue seeing me in three-month intervals, but six-month checkups were standard protocol in my case. I should have been jumping for joy, but I had grown accustomed to seeing my doctors on a regular basis and it made me feel safe. I had to get used to the fact that I would no longer be running from one doctor appointment to another, a sign I was well on my road to recovery.

35 JUANITA

Big Al could see I was not myself and he knew there was only one remedy to cheer me up. Road trip! He quickly planned a week-long excursion beginning with a ride up Interstate 5 to San Francisco, continuing along the coast of Northern California and Oregon and returning home with pit stops in Salem, Crater Lake and Mt. Shasta. The timing was ideal.

On Saturday October 10th, we threw some clothes in the car and off we went, with reservations for only the first two nights. The rest of the time we would wing it, staying in some fleabag joints along the way. One night I slept fully clothed with my Ugg boots on, afraid that bed bugs might attack at any moment. Big Al would say I'm exaggerating. We had not done anything that spontaneous since before we had our children. There is nothing like the freedom of hitting the open road to cure what ails you.

We laughed, we ate, we drank, we fought, we laughed some more and we rediscovered the intimacy we had been longing for. The first night in San Francisco we had dinner with my favorite niece, Michele, and her friend, Amy. Michele is my brother's only child and she is a remarkable young woman who has always had a soft spot in her heart for her Auntee Nicki. She used to visit us in the summers when she was a teenager and she became our third child.

Michele and Amy came down to visit me ten days after my mastectomies and hosted a small dinner party for us. Michele is a formally trained chef, so even in my stupor I enjoyed the delicious food. I was barely with the program, still out of it on pain meds, but recall how much I appreciated that precious time with my niece. Ally and Matt were away at school and she filled the void of their absence. Now it was five months later and I was a whole new woman. Our dinner in San Francisco was a sweet reminder of how far I had come.

The next few days Big Al and I meandered up the coast of Northern California, stopping for a sublime hike in Trinidad. I'm not sure why we chose to stop there, but we were drawn to the coastline. It was incredibly beautiful, with houses dotting the nearby hillside. When we reached the top of the path overlooking the Pacific we found ourselves staring at a cross that had been placed there in 1915. It had replaced the original monument erected in 1775. It was an unexpected moment on our trip, serving as a sign that wherever I went I was in God's hands.

Unfortunately, the weather did not cooperate as we traveled up the Oregon Coast. We spent the next couple of days battling high winds and rain, and finally settled in Lincoln City to ride out the storm. We stayed at a lovely small hotel on the beach. After surviving howling sixty-five mph winds the first night, we decided to get some exercise and take a walk. There was not a soul in sight as we strolled along the seven-mile stretch of sand. While I became engrossed in searching for shells, Alan kept himself busy taking pictures of the surf and seagulls.

Out of nowhere, through the mist, there appeared a woman in a bright pink jacket holding a walking stick while looking for shells. She was wearing a blue and white beanie with a fluffy little ball on top and a pair of wire rim glasses perched on her nose. I rarely look at someone so closely, but I studied her face, searching for clues about her life.

I was inexplicably drawn to her. I nodded at her and smiled. I was so glad when she stopped and asked me where I was from. She volunteered that she lived in Salem, just an hour and half away. She was visiting Lincoln City with her husband for a few days of R & R. She mentioned he was unable to walk long distances, but *she* enjoyed a three-mile walk every day. She volunteered that she was 80 years old and had just celebrated her mother's 101st birthday. I was astounded by their longevity, but completely floored by what she said next. Her mother was a fifty-one year breast cancer survivor.

Was I dreaming? There I stood on Lincoln City Beach, on October 14th, six months to the day of my bilateral mastectomy, and out of nowhere Juanita appeared with this inspiring story of survival. I did not tell Juanita I was a breast cancer survivor, but I know she sensed a kinship with me. We chatted for a few minutes before she went on her way. As I turned to walk in the opposite direction she said, "Excuse me. Why don't you take these two shells I found? I have so many of them. Think of them as mama and baby shells."

They were almost identical, but in different sizes. I thanked her for the sweet gesture and took the shells from her weathered hands. I will treasure them always.

When I turned to look for Big Al to tell him what had happened he admitted he had been snapping pictures of Juanita and me. I'm so glad he provided the proof that she really existed. I have never believed there are any coincidences in life. Things happen for a reason and I was meant to meet Juanita from Salem, to reassure me there is a life to be lived after breast cancer.

Six days and 2,000 miles after our road trip began, Big Al and I returned home, rejuvenated and reconnected. It was the best elixir in the world for us.

36 MUMBO JUMBO

I was initially reluctant to meet with Lisa Donley. I have always been a private person and never put a lot of credence in therapy. I thought it was just a bunch of psycho mumbo jumbo. In retrospect, it was something I should have considered years ago. I kept telling myself I just needed more time to heal. My friend, Kate, told me distance from my diagnosis was what I needed. Time would make things better. Big Al, however, was growing impatient because it did not appear to him that I wanted to help myself. He strongly suggested I join a survivor support group or talk to an expert who had an understanding of the psychological ramifications of breast cancer. I expected him to be more supportive and sensitive to my needs. I thought his suggestions had more to do with the fact that he was ready to move on and get back to doing the things he loves, never mind how I was feeling.

I finally gave in and made an appointment to see Lisa Donley the Monday after we returned from our road trip. I came up with every excuse in the book to cancel, but deep down inside I knew I needed help.

Lisa could not have been more empathetic. She is an expert at dealing with breast cancer survivors because she has the credentials, years of experience and is a survivor herself. That gave her instant credibility with me. I expressed my apprehension about not having chemo, revealing I had yet to meet another woman like myself who was node-positive and did not have chemotherapy; I felt like I was in a club of one. She explained in detail the science behind the Oncotype test, and told me I was a pioneer on the cutting edge of the latest technology used in analyzing breast cancer and determining the recommended treatment options for women like me. She told me I wasn't giving enough credit to Femara, a powerful drug which would do more for me in preventing a recurrence than chemo by blocking the estrogen production in my body and starving any remaining cancer cells. She drew diagrams, making everything plain and simple to me. When I told her I was a complete freak show on Femara she reiterated what Dr. Waisman had said. The side effects would diminish over time and I would begin feeling less volatile and out of sorts. The hot flashes, joint pain and sleeplessness should also subside.

When I shared my astonishing story with her regarding the devastation caused by the staggering amount of cancer in my family, she offered up some words of advice I will never forget.

She said, "Nicki, you have waited your whole life for the other shoe to drop. Now that it has, go buy yourself a new pair of shoes."

It instantly lightened the mood in the room and I envisioned my first pair of Manolos in my closet.

And then I told her about my epiphany. It wasn't easy relaying to a stranger what happened that day at the Church of the Good Shepherd and the profound effect it had on me. I wasn't sure she could understand. She listened intently, and I got the impression it was not the first time she heard a breast cancer patient talk about their newfound relationship with God. She said when someone has an epiphany she believes they should act on the revelation. It wouldn't be an epiphany if I didn't share my insight or effect positive change in my life in some way. She suggested I write, believing it would be cathartic for me.

I spent almost three hours with Lisa Donley and felt as though the weight of the world had been lifted from my shoulders. Big Al had been right. I did indeed need to talk to a professional to share my concerns and my darkest, in-the-night fears. One session and I felt as though I could breathe again. I drove home and thanked God for bringing another angel into my life.

37 BARN'S BURNT DOWN...

The next day I was having breakfast with an old friend from New York. We met thirty years before when were young adults with our whole lives ahead of us, filled with so much promise. I hadn't seen Stephen since I was diagnosed and I was nervous for some reason. I wanted to quickly get through the boring details of the past few months and talk about anything other than breast cancer. Stephen is a literary agent and movie producer and at the time his life was far more interesting than mine.

We met in Brentwood at Le Pain Quotidien and sat outside, lazily drinking our tea and coffee and enjoying one another's company. Stephen is one of the most insightful people I know. He is shockingly honest and never bullshits me. It was so good to see him and just chill for a couple of hours. He lifted my spirits and encouraged me with his sincere words and the kindness in his eyes. We are typically a laugh a minute, but that day we enjoyed each other on a much deeper level.

After we said goodbye, I stopped by the Pulp and Hide, a candy and card shop at the Brentwood Country Mart. I wanted to buy a thank you note for Lisa Donley. As I sorted through the carousels of cards I found one that took my breath away and would make everything crystal clear. It said, "barn's burnt down...now i can see the moon." I was unfamiliar with the quote, but would later find out it was a haiku written by the poet Masahide in the 17th century. The poet's profound words held significant meaning for me.

The barn represented my breast cancer and encompassed the sad memories I had stored for decades. Now that it had burned down, my perspective on life had changed. I was a survivor, who along the way had been transformed into a woman filled with grace. Out of the ashes rose the lessons learned and the love between a mother and daughter that will endure forever. I would find a safe place for my mother's wedding ring and let go of my grief at last.

I could no longer allow my past to block my view of the future, otherwise my journey would have been in vain. The shock of my diagnosis was a startling wake-up call to enjoy each day. With my eyes wide open, and my view unobstructed I could finally see the brilliant moon, imbued in pink, with the faces of all the women and men who have bravely walked before me.

I had been blessed with a second epiphany. It was time to share my enlightenment with others, time to write my story. Time to let go and live.

ACKNOWLEDGMENTS

Shortly after the conclusion of this book, I met Jennifer Veigel, another patient of Dr. Orringer. Jennifer wanted to see someone who had smaller implants, so I agreed to model the new twins. We clicked instantly and shortly thereafter started our own therapy group with a membership of two. Jennifer and I became each other's confidantes, sharing the ups and downs of our journeys and our innermost fears. Thank you Jennifer, for enriching my life and being my friend. You are an extraordinary young woman indeed and I am blessed to know you. Keep calm and carry on!

I wrote Beyond the Pink Moon as a personal catharsis, and to hopefully make a difference in the life of a breast cancer survivor. I never expected that survivor would be my editor, April L. Hamilton. I had read about April in a New York Times article my new friend, Deb Werner sent me about self-publishing. April is an independent editor who has received widespread acclaim. It took all of my nerve to write to her. You can imagine my astonishment when she wrote back and said she had just completed treatment for breast cancer two weeks before. I believe I have made a difference in her life and she in mine. Thank you April, for your top-notch editing skills, encouragement and patience. I know I'm an anal retentive freak, but I may have met my match in you.

There are a few people to whom I would like to extend my gratitude, beginning with my Aunt Lydia. Thank you for being my mother's beloved sister and best friend. You embody the heroic spirit of a survivor. Cousin Georgi, you are my rock! To my brother, Jerome A. Boscia, MD, better known as Jer or bro, we shared the same childhood, the same memories and the same DNA. You are more like me than any other person on the planet. Thanks for always having my back. To my sister-in-law, Diane, I still carry the rock you found on Fort Funston beach as a reminder to stay positive and healthy. We met the night of my high school graduation and I knew then you were the one for my bro. He's a lucky guy. To my niece Michele, thank you for making your Auntee feel so loved when I needed it the most. Your cooking revived me! To my brothers-in-law, Howard and Steven Durlester and their families, thank you for your love and support. And to my father-in-law, Ira, you will always be my fav!

I would like to thank my doctors for their care and compassion. I found that choosing a physician came down to chemistry. There are countless qualified doctors in the world, but credentials are not the only things that matter. I believe you should feel comfortable and encouraged by the women and men who diagnose and treat you. I would like to extend my gratitude to the following physicians: James Pritchard, Kristi Funk, Jay Orringer, Avrum Bluming, Jim Waisman, Eugene Fishman, William Cipriano, Peter-Brian Anderson, Mary Hardy, Mao Ni and Guy Armstrong. I am also grateful for the wonderful care I received from all the nurses who took care of me while I was at Cedars-Sinai and St.

John's. Lisa Donley, thank you for your sage advice and for encouraging me to write my story. Epiphany realized!

I would also like to extend my thanks to two doctors who were not on my team but were there to support me throughout my ordeal, Dr. Lori Migdal and Dr. Michael Levine. They are a dynamic husband and wife duo who made themselves available whenever Big Al and I needed dinner companions. Thanks for the hall passes on all the times I cancelled.

Jonathan Petuchowski and Leslie Yenkin were the first two people to read the beginning chapters of my book. Thank you for your early positive reviews. It motivated me to continue writing and finishing my story. Carla Friedman, I owe the title to you. The original one was The Pink Moon, but when April reminded me it was also the title of a famous song by Nick Drake, I knew I had to change it. Thank you Carla, for brainstorming with me and for being a true friend. Hash and Teri Greenblatt, you are our nearest and dearest friends. Time and distance will never change that. Jimmy and Susie Kay, thank you for your inspirational emails and for being a great support team for "son". To my long time business partner and close friend, Ford Roosevelt—Harry and Sally can't hold a candle to us and we proudly dispel the myth that a straight man and straight woman can't just be friends. We had a great run!

There are two individuals who held down the Durlester fort when I was overwhelmed. David DeLucca, thank you for not only maintaining our home, but for lifting me up with your prayers and encouragement. I will never forget your kindness. A big thank you to Rosa Saravia for quietly taking care of me during those dark days and for everything you've done for our family the past twenty-three years. I am deeply grateful for your care and loyalty.

And now, to the three most important people in my life...

My husband Alan Scott Durlester, better known as Big Al: you may only be 5'8" tall on a good day; however, you're a giant among men to me. We met when I was walking down the street carrying groceries and you asked me if I needed help. Thank God I said yes. I still believe my mother had something to do with that. You have stood by my side through better and worse, in sickness and in health. It was you and me all the way, not always pretty but 100% real, and a testimony to the commitment we made twenty-five years ago.

And my children, Ally Bianchina and Matthew Hunter: there are no words to tell you how much joy you have brought into my life. Ally, when you were born on your father's birthday and the day before my mother's, I knew you were a blessing from God and a message that life goes on. And Matthew, my baby bear, my boychick, you made our family complete. I am hugely grateful and proud of the remarkable young adults you and your sister have become.

Big Al, Ally and Matt, none of us knows what will happen in the future, but what I do know is that health and time are the real bling-bling of life. So take care of yourselves, drink green tea, treasure every day and know that our love for each other will endure forever. *Ti amo!*

AFTERWORD

Beyond the Pink Moon was published on July 30, 2010, my 54th birthday, 14 months after my bilateral mastectomy. What a difference a year made!

For the first time in my life I felt completely liberated from the overwhelming fear of getting breast cancer. Been there, done it and survived. Life seemed to back on autopilot.

I was in the middle of doing book signings when my 23-year-old daughter, Ally, announced she wanted to be tested for the BRCA2 gene. I asked her to wait a few years, knowing full well what the repercussions of the test result might be. But she insisted and had every right to know. This wasn't about me anymore.

Being the eternal optimist I had convinced myself Ally would be negative. She looked more like Big Al's family, had few of my characteristics and the onset and pattern of her menstrual cycle were completely different from my mother's and mine. These were the mental gymnastics I went through in order to convince myself I had not passed the legacy on to her.

I had hoped and prayed the gene would end with me. It did not. On October 11, 2010, Dr. Funk informed my only daughter that she had indeed tested positive for the BRCA2 gene. I was sitting on Ally's bed watching as she cleaned out her closet when her cell phone rang. She never skipped a beat. She looked up, shrugged her shoulders and said, "Mom, I'm positive."

My heart sank as I began to cry. Through my tears I said, "I am so sorry, Ally." But, she wasn't placing blame. Ally was characteristically strong while consoling me and as optimistic as she has always been.

She profoundly said, "Mom, the gene may not have ended with you, but breast cancer will. I refuse to sit around waiting for the other shoe to drop."

Without judgment, Ally has learned from the steps I missed and the decisions I made. She is certain she will have prophylactic mastectomies and oophorectomies when the time is right for her. In the meantime, with an excellent team of doctors including Dr. Kristi Funk and her gynecologist, Dr. Jessica Schneider, she will practice vigilant active surveillance.

It will take time for me to come to terms with the magnitude and guilt of being a gene carrier and passing it on to my daughter. I take comfort, however, in knowing that Ally will take all the necessary steps to stay healthy and live a long active life. She has all the benefit of hindsight. For that I am grateful.

MammaPrint and Oncotype DX

The source for the Oncotype DX information provided in this book is a brochure entitled *Make Oncotype DX Part of the Conversation*. More information about Oncotype DX can be found at the Oncotype DX website: http://www.oncotypeDX.com.

The source for the MammaPrint information provided in this book is a brochure entitled *MammaPrint decoding breast cancer*. MammaPrint is the registered trademark of Agendia. More information about MammaPrint can be found at the Agendia website: http://www.agendia.com.

Made in the USA
Lexington, KY
07 September 2011